If Found

This workbook holds many thoughts and ideas that I am grateful to have had. I would be thankful if you returned this workbook to me:

Name:

Address:

Phone:

Email:

Why You Should Read
The Beginner's Guide to Psychedelics

"In my decades of exploring psychedelics' potential to expand and heal human consciousness, I've seen the importance of guidance for their safe and responsible use. The Beginner's Guide to Psychedelics provides clear, thoughtful direction for newcomers looking to explore the healing and transformative power of psychedelics, from microdosing to ceremonial practices. For those curious and ready to take this journey, this book is a trusted companion back to wholeness and meaning."

-James Fadiman, PhD, Psychedelic Researcher, and author (with Jordan Gruber) of Microdosing for Health, Healing, and Enhanced Performance

"At Heroic Hearts Project, we've seen how psychedelics can help veterans reclaim their lives, breaking free from trauma and despair where other treatments fall short. But this healing isn't just for veterans- it's for anyone seeking a deeper understanding of themselves and a new way forward. In The Beginner's Guide to Psychedelics, Matt Zemon distills complex science, ancient wisdom, and modern best practices into a clear, accessible guide that demystifies the journey."

-Jesse Gould, Founder and President, Heroic Hearts Project
Former Army Ranger

"A rich resource for those curious about the healing and transformative potential of psychedelics. Drawing on decades of research and collective wisdom, and including necessary cautions, The Beginner's Guide to Psychedelics provides a structured yet flexible framework for using these substances more safely to explore one's inner landscape."

-Bob Jesse, Guiding force behind the contemporary re-emergence of psychedelics and co-author of foundational research at Johns Hopkins

"Psychedelics have the power to cut through layers of disconnection and emotional pain, going straight to the core of what truly needs healing. For those new to this journey, it's not just about managing symptoms—it's about processing, integrating, and moving beyond what holds us back. The Beginner's Guide to Psychedelics offers a clear and thoughtful roadmap to explore these powerful tools with safety, intention, and the promise of transformation."

-Dr Julie Holland, MD, Psychiatrist and Author of Good Chemistry

"The Beginner's Guide to Psychedelics is a wonderful resource for those ready to explore the therapeutic and transformative potential of these ancient medicines. This guide thoughtfully weaves together traditional ethnobotanical knowledge with modern insights, offering a risk-reduced and accessible path to healing and self-discovery."

-Dr. Dennis McKenna, PhD, President and Principal Founder of the McKenna Academy of Natural Philosophy, ethnopharmacologist, and founding Board member of the Heffter Research Institute

"For centuries, plant medicines have been revered as powerful tools for healing, transformation, and connection. The Beginner's Guide to Psychedelics provides a bridge back to these ancient traditions, helping readers safely and thoughtfully engage with nature's most profound teachers. This guide offers a clear and compassionate path for those seeking to explore psychedelics as a means of healing, self-discovery, and growth."

-Bia Labate, PhD, Anthropologist and Expert on Plant Medicines, Founder Chacruna

"Throughout my 20-year career researching psychedelics for mental health and addiction, I have witnessed the profound benefits these substances can provide when used responsibly with the right support and setting. At the same time, it is essential to acknowledge the risks. While psychedelics may not help everyone, many find them transformative. *The Beginner's Guide to Psychedelics* empowers individuals to approach these medicines safely and thoughtfully, making it an excellent resource for those seeking new avenues for healing and growth."

-Dr. Matthew W. Johnson, PhD, Senior Researcher at Sheppard Pratt Center of Excellence for Psilocybin Research and Treatment

"*The Beginner's Guide to Psychedelics* is an invitation to reclaim self-agency and step into the transformative potential of psychedelics. This guide goes beyond healing—it's about awakening to a more integrated, liberated, and authentic life. For those ready to embark on this journey, this book offers the wisdom and tools needed to navigate it with intention and clarity."

-Susan Guner, Holistic Psychotherapist, Host of Psychedelic Conversations Podcast, RESET Microdosing Integration Program

"In the Jewish tradition, we are taught the moral imperative to care for those in need of healing. The Beginner's Guide to Psychedelics answers that sacred call, providing a compassionate, accessible, and spiritually grounded resource for individuals exploring psychedelic medicines. As someone whose ancestors might have benefited from this work, I am proud to endorse this guide as a powerful companion for those seeking transformation, connection, and renewal."

-Rabbi Zac Kamenetz, Founder and CEO of Shefa:
A Jewish Psychedelic Society

"My experience in a psilocybin clinical trial revealed the profound healing and spiritual growth that these sacred substances can offer, affirming the deep interconnection between mental and spiritual well-being. The Beginner's Guide to Psychedelics invites anyone seeking wholeness to explore this transformative path with care and reverence. This guide is a true blessing, offering a bridge beyond pain and disconnection into the transformative power of the Divine."

-Hunt Priest, Episcopal Priest, Founding Director of Ligare:
A Christian Psychedelic Society

"There is tremendous potential in the use of psychedelics, which I have witnessed firsthand and which is supported by a growing body of research. However, these experiences are most effective when approached with preparation and support. The Beginner's Guide to Psychedelics provides the education and awareness needed to make informed decisions and safely embark on this transformative path.

-Neil Markey, CEO & Co-Founder Beckley Retreats, US Army Veteran

"Psychedelics and music have a powerful connection in fostering healing and transformation. Resources like The Beginner's Guide to Psychedelics are valuable for those exploring how these tools can support growth, connection, and recovery in the psychedelic space."

-East Forest, Musician and Producer

"As a psychopharmacologist specializing in psychedelics, I often emphasize the importance of informed decision-making and harm reduction when exploring these substances. The Beginner's Guide to Psychedelics provides readers with the tools to approach psychedelics thoughtfully, emphasizing risk reduction and optimization through preparation, safety, and integration."

-Dr. Ben Malcolm (The Spirit Pharmacist), PharmD, MPH

"Just as mushrooms and other psychedelics have transformed my life, they hold the potential to unlock profound healing and growth for so many others. The Beginner's Guide to Psychedelics offers a clear and thoughtful roadmap for newcomers, helping them explore this path with intention and safety, guiding them toward a brighter, more empowered future."

Alli Schaper, CEO Into the Multiverse, Co-Founder Microdosing Collective

"The Beginner's Guide to Psychedelics offers a gentle and heartfelt process for those ready to explore the healing power of psychedelics. With deep wisdom and care, this guide provides the tools to approach psychedelic experiences with intention, safety, and reverence. It honors the courage it takes to embark on this journey of transformation and offers support in reconnecting to one's strength, wholeness, and inner light. This book is a true act of love, guiding readers toward healing, self-discovery, and peace."

Spring Washam, Co-Founder, Spirit Underground Liberation Project, Author *The Spirit of Harriet Tubman*

"The Beginner's Guide to Psychedelics is a practical and empowering roadmap for anyone interested in exploring these transformative tools for healing and growth. Thoughtfully crafted and very accessible, this guide provides the essential knowledge and insights needed to navigate the psychedelic journey with confidence and care."

Joe Moore, CEO at Psychedelics Today

"For far too long, those suffering from trauma—whether from combat, personal loss, injury or life's (and particularly childhood's) many unseen--or repressed-- battles—have been offered so-called, evidenced-based trauma treatments. These interventions often manage and mitigate symptoms of trauma and stress but fail to heal truly. As a holistic physician and integrative psychiatrist dedicated to addressing the hidden wounds of war, I understand that healing must go beyond symptom relief; it must mend the whole person, including the body, spirit, and mind. Used properly and with adequate preparation, and individualized care, psychedelic-assisted therapies have the potential to repair not just the province of the mental health provider, but importantly, liberate the chains of moral injury, and restore the soul, too. In The Beginner's Guide to Psychedelics, Matt Zemon provides an invaluable resource for anyone ready to embark on a life-altering journey towards true liberation and total healing."

-Robert Koffman, MD, MPH, Captain, MC, USN (ret.)

"With the growing wave of information on best practices for psychedelic use, Matt Zemon takes it a step further by compiling all the essential resources, years of research, and wisdom into one accessible guide for those looking to navigate psychedelics safely and intentionally. As a community and political organizer, I frequently meet people who are just beginning to explore the topic of psychedelics, and I'm grateful to have a comprehensive resource to point them to. The Beginner's Guide to Psychedelics is a must-read for anyone looking to optimize the psychedelic experience and catalyze themselves towards deep, personal transformation."

-Gina Giorgio, Director of Strategy and Development,
Students for Sensible Drug Policy

"As a conflict journalist and military spouse, I've seen the deep scars trauma leaves—not just on veterans, but on people from all walks of life. Psychedelics hold immense potential for healing, but they are not a shortcut to recovery. True transformation requires knowledge, preparation, and integration. The Beginner's Guide to Psychedelics offers exactly that—a clear, accessible, and responsible framework for anyone considering these medicines. This book isn't just about psychedelics; it's about reclaiming hope, restoring wholeness, and making meaningful healing accessible to those who need it most."

-AnneClaire Stapleton, Two-time Emmy and DuPont Award-Winning
Conflict Journalist, Military Spouse, Advocate for Psychedelic-Assisted
Therapy and Veteran Mental Health

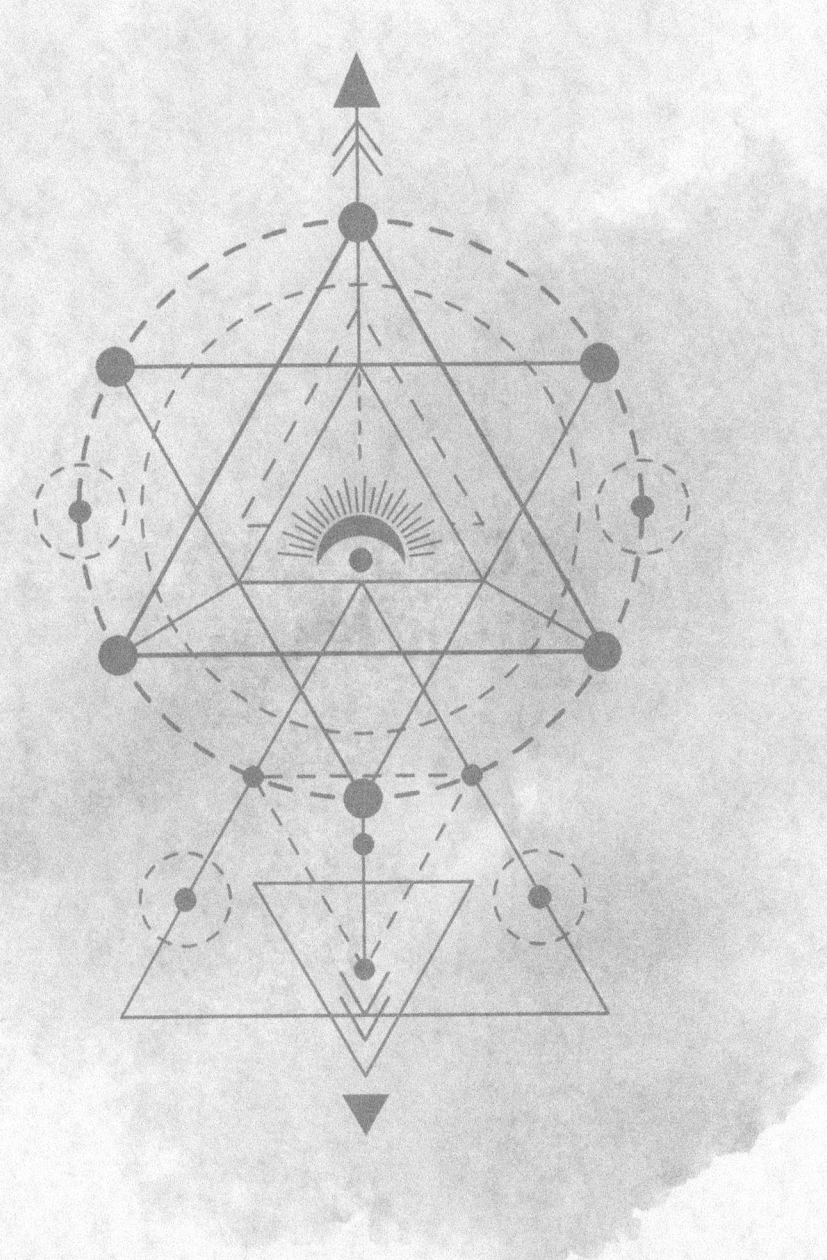

YOU are the
medicine

THE BEGINNER'S GUIDE TO PSYCHEDELICS

HOW TO REDUCE RISK, DEEPEN CONNECTION, AND MAXIMIZE INSIGHTS

Matt Zemon, MSc

Foreword by William A Richards, STM, PhD

Clinically reviewed by Ken Weingardt, PhD

PSYCHED

PUBLISHING

Published by Psyched Publishing.
All rights reserved.

Copyright © 2024 by Matt Zemon
Foreword © 2024 by William A Richards

Name: Matt Zemon, author
Title: The Beginner's Guide To Psychedelics: *How to Reduce Risk, Deepen Connection, and Maximize Insights*
Clinically reviewed by: Ken Weingardt, PhD
Edited by: Melissa Gedachian Zemon
Identifiers:
ISBN: 979-8-9918940-0-5 (Hardcover)
ISBN: 979-8-9918940-1-2 (Paperback)
First printed edition: 2025

Bulk copies can be ordered at:

www.mattzemon.com/beginners

The foreword with minor edits originally appeared in Voices. Copyright 2024 American Academy of Psychotherapists (AAP). All rights reserved. Reprinted with permission of Voices: The Art and Science of Psychotherapy and the American Academy of Psychotherapists, from Vol. 60 Nos. 1-3, 2024.

Portions of this workbook were originally created with Wolf Shlagman for HAPPŸŸ and are used with permission. I am grateful to Wolf for his generosity of spirit, his passion for the transformational power of psychedelic medicine, and his belief in the human promise.

DISCLAIMER

This book relates to the authors' research on best practices related to the preparation and integration of psychedelic journeys. Neither the writer nor the publisher can be held accountable for any physical, psychological, or legal outcomes that may arise from consuming psychedelic substances.

It is a criminal offense in the United States and many other countries, punishable by imprisonment and/or fines, to manufacture, possess, or supply some of these medicines. This book is therefore intended to provide readers with information but does not encourage illegal activity, including but not limited to the unlawful sale, purchase, or use of controlled substances.

Please do not treat this book as medical advice, diagnosis, or treatment. Talk to your medical provider about your specific health-related questions. Never disregard professional medical advice or delay in seeking it because of something you have read in this book.

For Melissa- I am so grateful for your love, patience, support, and insight.

DEDICATION

This book is dedicated to the indigenous communities spanning the globe, who have preserved the sacred knowledge and traditions of psychedelic medicines through countless generations. It also honors those seekers who embark on the journey of inner exploration and connection with the mysteries, trusting the power of these sacred medicines.

"Reflect on the mysterious truth that, if you turn your attention inward, you can become aware that you are aware. When you do so, an indisputable and profound inner knowing arises that is at the core of our humanity: We recognize that we are all in this together, and an impulse for mutual caretaking arises. I believe that exploration of this inner knowing through contemplative and other spiritual practices can result in a profound, uplifting shift in worldview; a waking up to a sense of freedom, peace, joy, and gratitude that many people simply find unimaginable."

-Roland Griffiths, Ph.D.
Johns Hopkins University

TABLE OF CONTENTS

FOREWORD

A Journey with Psychedelics: Reflections from a Life of Exploration

ONCE UPON A TIME, I WAS A 23-YEAR-OLD GRADUATE STUDENT who had left the Yale Divinity School for a year of study in Germany at the University of Göttingen. Not only were psychedelics legal and uncontroversial at that time, I had yet to hear the word psychedelic and had no idea what psilocybin might be. I was, however, committed to the development of my own psychological and spiritual life, even to the extent of going without breakfast on some days to record my dreams from the night before.

Two of my new friends told me about an interesting research project going on in the Nervenklinik (mental hospital) around the corner from my dormitory. It entailed receiving some new drug that was purported to give access to memories from early childhood. One friend reported a vivid memory of sitting on his father's lap, which was profoundly meaningful as his father had been killed in World War II. The other claimed to have seen a hallucination of SS men marching in the streets. I had never seen a real hallucination, so this sounded intriguing. Curious about my early childhood psychodynamics, notably my oedipal complex, I hiked over to the clinic and inquired whether I also could participate in the research project.

I was given a cursory medical interview to establish that I was in decent mental and physical health and didn't get drunk too often, declared acceptable, and then led to a small basement room, dim and drab, with a cot, an end-table and a narrow window overlooking the hospital garbage cans. There a friendly medical intern about my age, wearing a spiffy white coat and stethoscope, gave me an injection of a short-acting derivative of psilocybin (13 mg. of CZ-74), and, though looking in on me periodically, basically left me alone for the next 4 hours.

Drawing on the piety of my Methodist childhood, I affirmed trust that God would be with me if any potentially traumatic memories awakened. I then became aware of very beautiful neon-like geometrical designs in my visual field, multi-dimensional, unfolding, and inviting my participation in and through energetic forces that flowed through them.

1

They reminded me of Islamic architecture and Arabic script. Gradually, yet suddenly, my usual state of consciousness in the everyday world merged into the vivid transcendental awareness we now call mystical consciousness-an eternal state of being that felt more real (or fundamental) than my usual awareness, filled with beauty, joy, love, and intuitive knowledge that seemed independent of time and space. Awestruck, I (my usual sense of ego/self) underwent what we call psychological death and rebirth.

In the midst of this unexpected epiphany, as workmen emptied the metal garbage cans outside of the window, I registered tinkling temple bells. When the intern entered, asking me to sit up on the edge of the cot so he could test my knee reflexes, I complied with thoughts of compassion for the infancy of science. Now, 60 years later, I realize that in many ways my subsequent personal and professional life has been footnotes to this unexpected awakening. It led to study of the psychology of religion, comparative religions, music, and clinical psychology. I found myself pursuing research with psychedelics in Göttingen in 1964, in Boston in 1966 (Pahnke & Richards, 1966), and then at the Spring Grove Hospital Center (which morphed into the Maryland Psychiatric Research Center) from 1967-1977 (Richards et al., 1972; Richards et al., 1977; Rhead et al., 1977; Richards & Rhead, 1977). Psychedelic research in the United States then became dormant until dimethyltryptamine (DMT) studies began in the early 1990s (Strassman, 2001). In 1999, Roland Griffiths and I were able to initiate its rebirth with psilocybin at the Johns Hopkins School of Medicine (Griffiths, et al., 2006, 2008, 2011, & 2017; Johnson, et al., 2008; Garcia-Romeu & Richards, 2018), where it continues to this day. I now also contribute to psychedelic research at Sunstone Therapies in Rockville, Maryland (Agrawal et al., 2023). Throughout these decades of career research, I have often reflected upon that first psychedelic experience.

When Matt asked me to contribute a piece of writing as a foreword to The Beginner's Guide to Psychedelics, I thought about what I could offer that would be most valuable to those stepping onto this path for the first time. During my journey, I have had the opportunity to participate in the implementation of studies using LSD, DPT, MDA, MDMA and psilocybin, both with well-functioning mental health and religious professionals and with persons suffering from addictions to alcohol or narcotics, depression, anxiety, and other forms of psychological distress, notably cancer patients coming to terms with the lives they have lived and the approach of death.

During approximately 38 years of research activity, my colleagues and I have experienced the privilege of working in significant depth with a rich variety of persons: adult men and women aged between early 20s and mid-80s from different educational, occupational, and racial/cultural backgrounds. Most were encountered in the context of individual psychotherapy, though some participated in ayahuasca groups in South America or, recently, group interventions with cancer patients. From this vantage point, I offer the following perspectives and recommendations. As you continue into the heart of this book, you'll find exercises related to many of these. I hope the insights shared here and within are helpful to you on your path.

The Critical Importance of Interpersonal Grounding

There is no question that risk-reduced and effective experiences with psychedelic substances almost always require more than simply receiving a drug or piece of blotter paper, drinking a tea, or chewing on some plant material. The psychedelic molecule may indeed provide an opportunity, giving access to a vast array of alternative forms of human consciousness, but how one responds to that opportunity depends not only on the molecular structure, dosage, and purity of substance but also on the recipient's ability to choose to relinquish the usual controls of the ego and to enter into the experiences choreographed by his/her own mind regardless of their nature and content. In research settings, for decades, this attitude has been encouraged with the mantram, "Trust, let go, and be open" (TLO). This decisive, courageous attitude for most persons seems to be most easily expressed in the context of a human relationship where a significant degree of unconditional acceptance and support has been established. This is especially critical in sessions with moderate or high dosage when the recipient may feel as though he/she is dying or going crazy as transitions in consciousness are occurring. If one seeks to escape from the emerging experiential content or to somehow censor or control it, the "nightmare sequence" usually occurs, typified by fear, panic, confusion, and sometimes paranoia. Such bad trips are extremely rare when an effective therapeutic alliance has been established in advance.

There appears to be a profound principle being expressed in the therapeutic alliance, often acknowledged in concepts such as the bejeweled net of Indra in Hinduism or the brotherhood of man or family of humanity in Western religious thought.

Viewed as more fundamental than the usual everyday awareness of most of us, this sense of belonging or inter-connectedness within the mind, though often forgotten, remains a common discovery when mystical forms of consciousness are becoming manifested. In the framework of transpersonal psychology, one might note that in Latin trans means both above/beyond and between/across. When a person thinks, "I can do this on my own and don't really need anybody," some psychedelic sessions may prove to be safe and perhaps life-enhancing, but eventually it appears probable that very challenging content will eventually emerge and be difficult to explore in constructive ways without interpersonal grounding. In my own experience, my introduction to psychedelic experiences described above was indeed positive and occurred without an established therapeutic alliance. I would note that my mental state at the time was one of openness, that I chose to trust/entrust, and that the dosage happened to be relatively low. Yet, in a subsequent experience under similar conditions I experienced acute psychological distress which, though intellectually instructive as an experiential seminar in psychosis and paranoia, did not prove to be facilitative of personal development.

Preparatory Psychoeducation

Just as if one were to go skiing or scuba-diving for the first time, it is wise and sometimes imperative to receive some basic instruction on how to navigate within alternative states of consciousness before embarking on a psychedelic-assisted journey. Such instruction is easily provided; it frames the psychological set that maximizes the positive, healing potential of psychedelic-assisted excursions into the mind. It also enhances the therapeutic bond. The essence of such preparatory instruction is expressed in the following six principles or guidelines:

1) *Being present, accepting, and exploring the content that emerges,* irrespective of its nature. During the period of psychedelic-assisted access to mental processes, many different experiences may occur. Some may be beautiful and inspiring; others may entail suffering, perhaps involving the confrontation and reliving of trauma or intense encounters with guilt, shame, fear, anger, or unresolved grief. My impression is that each human mind is endowed with a certain wisdom that knows how to best choreograph the emergence and resolution of conflicts and healing processes. The task of the therapist or entheogenic guide is to be a facilitator, akin to a midwife who supports the person as emergence occurs, not to be a mechanic intent on fixing or repairing with various interventions.

4

Thus, the person who receives the psychedelic is supported in exploring and valuing whatever may emerge rather than judging whether it is good or bad, interesting or boring, transcendental or mundane, etc. The motivation for using a psychedelic to potentially accelerate and deepen the therapeutic process is expressed in a willingness to move into and through any suffering that may be encountered as an intrinsic part of an acknowledged desire for personal and perhaps spiritual development. From this perspective, the dark night of the soul, as expressed by St. John of the Cross in the 16th century, is not a symptom of failure or a distraction but rather an intrinsic part of the spiritual journey.

2) *Readiness to rapidly confront* any manifestations within the field of awareness that appear potentially frightening is of fundamental importance. If a monster/dragon/ bogeyman appears, one is prepared to meet it, perhaps acknowledging initial fear but then asserting curiosity and a desire for understanding: "Are you ever scary! But, why are you here? Where did you come from? What are you made of? What might I learn from you?" One is prepared to dive into the pupil of the eye if the threatening image has eyes, akin to diving into a swimming pool. The assumption is that it is your very own monster and that it appears in order to teach you something intrinsic to the healing process. In the religions that employ ayahuasca (South American psychoactive brew) there is the tradition of confronting the great anaconda serpent if it should appear. If one tries to flee and escape from it, panic and paranoia will reliably occur. Rather, one dives into its mouth and looks out through its eyes. In becoming the anaconda, perhaps one owns his/her own shakti (cosmic energy or life force: kundalini, elan vital, chi, etc.) and affirms/accepts the strength, empowerment, and creativity that the symbolic image may manifest.

Another metaphor for teaching this attitude that has been employed in many psychedelic research sites is the invitation to imagine going into the basement of one's life. One boldly announces, "I'm coming down," and descends with one firm step after the other, carrying a bright search-lamp, and perhaps affirming trust in the company of the therapist. One searches out the darkest corners one can find and brightly illuminates them, essentially affirming, "If there's anything down here that's contributing to my anxiety or depression, I want to know what it is." This proactive, courageous intention typically leads through abreaction but eventually culminates in an awareness that there is nothing to fear.

3) *Turning off the intellect* can be especially challenging for well-educated persons who tend to rely on the defense mechanism of intellectualization. A common response to the opportunities afforded by the action of a psychedelic substance is essentially to say to oneself, "Stop! What's going on here? Let me find some concepts, words, or labels to console myself before venturing any more deeply into my mind." This is the point at which some persons, if wearing an eyeshade, may lift its edges to reorient themselves in the room.

An established way to prepare for this defensive tendency is to essentially bribe the intellect in advance, perhaps on the day prior to the psychedelic experience. Essentially one says, "You're a wonderful intellect, so bright and clever. You guided me through graduate school and into my profession and have such a rich vocabulary. However, during the action of the psychedelic, you go out and play. I promise that, when you come back in at the end of the day, there will be many new experiences to reflect upon. At that time, you can draw on your knowledge of depth psychology, comparative religions, philosophy, and even quantum physics and choose the words that you find most helpful as you articulate and begin to integrate your experiences."

As classically expressed by the psychologist of religion, Rudolf Otto (1917), our mental processes may be viewed in three categories: the rational, the irrational, and the nonrational. It is this third category, often called intuition, that best reflects the most profound insights that occur in some psychedelic sessions. It is expressed well in verse from the Taoist scriptures, the Tao Te Ching: "Those who know do not speak; those who speak do not know."

4) Accepting and exploring somatic sensations may not only decrease potential physical discomfort, but may facilitate the encounter with and resolution of important psychological content. As has become increasingly recognized by therapists who specialize in the resolution of trauma, memories, and concomitant emotions often appear to be stored within or correlated with muscular tensions. If one focuses upon a particular. sensation that seems to be demanding attention, often a memory will awaken, and a sequence of potential resolution will occur. As well expressed by Bessel van der Kolk (2014), "The body keeps the score."

Thus a sensation that seems to command attention may be much more than an undesirable side-effect of a psychedelic substance; it may be an invitation to insight and healing.

Practically, this orientation is often helpful when dealing with nausea, perhaps the most common psychosomatic symptom that may occur during a psychedelic experience. One is instructed in advance that, should nausea occur, one should immediately "dive into her/his stomach"; when the sensation is accepted, it often immediately vanishes. Should the sensation be persistent and one reports a need to spit something out, experienced facilitators will invite the person who has ingested the psychedelic to briefly sit up and vomit/spit into an emesis basin, held at the person's mouth, typically without even removing the eyeshade or headphones if they are already in place. It is no big deal, and there's no need to interrupt the session to attend to the transient symptom.

Sometimes, as is recognized in communities that employ ayahuasca or peyote, the purgation is experienced as cleansing or purification, even to the extent of La Purga (vomiting and diarrhea together). When one lies back down, the inner journey continues to open up, and the somatic distress is left behind. It is noteworthy that with well-prepared persons nausea often doesn't occur at all. When it appears it often may be understood as a symptom of anxiety and an attempt of the everyday self (ego) to resist or control emerging content.

5) *Normalizing physical contact,* which may be sought for reassurance, connection, or occasionally for safety, is an important part of preparation. Demonstrated, discussed, and rehearsed, usually on the day prior to the session, it may provide potent interpersonal grounding especially during unexpectedly rapid transitions in consciousness or the emergence of challenging psychological content. It may supplement the steady, reassuring voice of the facilitator. Usually limited to reaching out for the hand of the facilitator or accepting a touch on the shoulder or arm, such connection for many persons can provide the nonverbal support required to channel anxiety constructively and encounter psychological content that otherwise might remain inaccessible.

This good touch can sometimes be of critical importance; although the body on the couch may look the same throughout the day, the content being experienced may range from that of a pre-verbal infant through many stages of development, even to the unitive consciousness of a spiritual master. Such human warmth and spontaneity can be communicated sensitively and effectively. The person who has received the psychedelic can reach out at any time and the facilitator can initiate supportive touch when his/her intuition prompts such behavior. Touch is never sexual; sessions may be video-recorded in settings where legal back-up or supervision is desired.

6) *Entering into music* that has been thoughtfully selected to provide nonverbal support, especially during the initial ascent and the most intense portions of a medium or high-dose session, may well significantly enhance the safety and efficacy of a psychedelic experience. Generally, the use of a well-designed playlist that has been found effective with diverse people is wise as it frees up the facilitator from playing disc jockey and enables the person to be more fully present with the psychedelic voyager. The usual musical preferences of either facilitator or voyager may not be important during the intense phases of a session, especially when the sound is experienced as a vehicle of transport and support and when consciousness has expanded beyond the usual limits of everyday awareness. Critique of music may be a common defense, especially when potentially stressful content is emerging during a session. When one is encouraged to "hate it with passion," resolution of conflicts tends to occur, and the very same music may be experienced as beautiful (Richards, 2022).

Concluding Comments

Although the use of psychedelics by humans may be traced to 9000 BC, if not to the dawn of civilization, and (like mushrooms) has appeared and vanished in many societies over time, they are now on the verge of integration into Western cultures in medical, educational, and religious contexts (Richards, 2016). The hope I share with many is that this integration will proceed in fundamentally safe and responsible ways.

Different people may well require different degrees of preparation, session guidance, and integrative support. Some with severe conditions of poor mental health may require extensive relationship-building and guidance in order to potentially experience the effects of psychedelics in beneficial ways and may be well advised to focus on milder meditative, psychotherapeutic, or psychopharmacological approaches of personal or spiritual development. Continuing research will help establish if, when, and how psychedelics may prove helpful to persons with significant psychotic tendencies or histories. However, we already have substantial data that are supportive of their beneficial use with a variety of mental health conditions. Further, they may well become recognized as powerful educational tools as we continue to explore the nature and mysteries of human consciousness. Their potential role in what we call religion or spirituality is being increasingly recognized. As Abraham Maslow (1966) stressed during the birth of humanistic and transpersonal psychology, true science is on the frontiers of knowledge, stretching to attempt to incorporate new concepts and language, which is where we find ourselves in psychedelic research.

Throughout these decades of career research, I have often reflected upon that first psychedelic experience. It is my hope that the readers of The Beginner's Guide to Psychedelics, standing at the threshold of their own explorations, will find similar moments of grace, discovery, and renewal. As I write these words, I feel a sense of kinship with those who will hold this book in their hands. May it light your path as you journey into the ever-deepening knowledge of the incredible miracle of your own being, just as my experience in that small room in Göttingen illuminated mine.

-Bill Richards

William A (Bill) Richards, STM, PhD, author of Sacred Knowledge and clinical psychologist, has contributed to psychedelic research since 1963. From 1967-1977, he implemented projects at the Maryland Psychiatric Research Center; in 1999, he and Roland Griffiths initiated the rebirth of research with psilocybin at the Johns Hopkins School of Medicine, which now has morphed into the Johns Hopkins Center for Psychedelic and Consciousness Research. Currently he focuses on integrating psychedelic therapy into palliative care at Sunstone Therapies.

References

Agrawal, M., Richards, W., Beaussant, Y., Shnayder, S., Ameli, R., Roddy, K., Stevens, N., Richards, B., Schor, N., Honstein, H., Jenkins, B., Bates, M., & Thambi, P. (2023). Psilocybin-assisted group therapy with cancer diagnosed with a major depressive disorder. Cancer, 130 (7), 1137-1146.

Garcia-Romeu, A., & Richards, W. (2018). Current perspectives on psychedelic therapy: Use of serotonergic hallucinogens in clinical interventions. International Review of Psychiatry 30(4), 291-316.

Griffiths, R., Richards, W., McCann, U., & Jesse, R. (2006). Psilocybin can occasion mystical-type experiences having substantial and sustained personal meaning and spiritual significance. Psychopharmacology, 187(3), 268-283.

Griffiths, R., Richards, W., Johnson, M., McCann, U., & Jesse, R. (2008). Mystical-type experiences occasioned by psilocybin mediate the attribution of personal meaning and spiritual significance 14 months later. Journal of Psychopharmacology, 22, 621-632.

Griffiths, R., Johnson, M., Richards, W., Richards B., McCann, U., & Jesse R. (2011). Psilocybin occasioned mystical-type experiences: Immediate and persisting dose-related effects. Psychopharmacology, 218,649-665.

Griffiths, R., Johnson, M., Richards, W., Richards, B., Jesse, R., MacLean K., Barrett, F., Cosimano, M., & Klinedinst, M. (2017). Psilocybin-occasioned mystical-type experiences in combination with meditation and other spiritual practices produces enduring positive changes in psychological functioning and trait measures of prosocial attitudes and behavior, Journal of Psychopharmacology, 32(1), 49-69.

Johnson, M., Richards, W., & Griffiths, R. (2008). Human hallucinogen research: Guidelines for safety. Journal of Psychopharmacology, 22, 603-619.

Maslow, A. (1966). The psychology of science: A reconnaissance. NY: Harper & Row.

Otto, R. (1917/1932). The idea of the holy. NY: Galaxy.

Rhead, J., Soskin, R., Turek, I., Richards, W., Yensen, R., Kurland, A., & Ota, K. (1977). Psychedelic drug (DPT)-assisted psychotherapy with alcoholics: A controlled study. Journal of Psychedelic Drugs, 9, 287-300.

Pahnke, W., & Richards, W. (1966). Implications of LSD and experimental mysticism. Journal of Religion and Health, 5, 175-208.

Richards, W., Grof, S., Goodman, L., & Kurland, A. (1972). LSD-assisted psychotherapy and the Human Encounter with Death. Journal of Transpersonal Psychology, 4, 121-150.

Richards, W., Rhead, J., DiLeo, F., Yensen, R., & Kurland, A. (1977). The peak experience variable in DPT-assisted psychotherapy with cancer patients. Journal of Psychedelic Drugs, 9, 1-10.

Richards, W., & Rhead, J. (1977). Psychedelic drug-assisted psychotherapy: Present perspectives, promises and problems. Journal of Altered States of Consciousness, 3, 97-98.

Richards W. (2016). Sacred knowledge: Psychedelics and religious experiences. NY: Columbia University Press.

Richards, W. (2022). Music in psychedelic research: The continuing legacy of Helen Bonny. Journal of the Association for Music and Imagery, 18, 83-93.

Strassman, R. (2001). The spirit molecule. Rochester: Park Street Press.
Van der Kolk, B. (2014). The body keeps the score. NY: Penguin Books.

Van der Kolk, B. (2014). The body keeps the score. NY: Penguin Books.

INTRODUCTION

I was 22 when my mom died- she was just 49. I felt like a part of my heart had been torn away, leaving behind a deep emptiness. Have you ever cried so hard you couldn't breathe? I didn't know I was capable of that kind of depth of sadness. And then, life moved on, as it does for the living.

Fast forward more than twenty years. Some friends invited me to participate in a guided magic mushroom journey. I am a responsible person—a business owner, a parent, a spouse. This isn't the kind of thing that fits into my world, yet something inside me said yes. And what happened next was beyond anything I could have imagined.

Suddenly, I melted into the earth. Everything around me—the ground, the sky, the trees—felt alive, connected. And for the first time in forever, I felt unconditionally loved.

And then, my mom was there- I could feel her. It was like I could pull a string from her to me and to my children. I could see that we were all carrying each other forward. I came out of this experience and wondered, "what the hell was that?" And I knew I had to learn more.

I went back to school to study psychedelic medicine and traveled the world to work with respected practitioners—Taitas, shamans, doctors, and researchers. What I uncovered on this journey was that having an incredibly meaningful experience with psychedelics was not uncommon and that psychedelics were *catalysts*, and not cures. Let me explain.

In a study from Johns Hopkins University, 77.8% of participants who took psilocybin, the active ingredient in the magic mushrooms that I took, described the experience as one of the five most meaningful moments in their lives.[1] More than half described it as THE most meaningful. What is important to understand is that this meaning wasn't *given* to the participants by the psychedelic. The meaning *came from* the participant, *enabled* by the psychedelic.

12

I now spend my days working closely with both medical professionals and spiritual leaders, all using psychedelics for healing, expanding consciousness, and personal growth. In this book we are going to discuss a few different psychedelics, some of the settings in which they are taken, and best practices for the process.

Before we dive too far into this, I need to be clear about a few things:

- First, while I have a Masters in psychology and neuroscience of mental health, I am not a medical doctor, and nothing I say should be construed as medical advice.

- Second, I am not advocating for anyone to engage in illegal activities or use psychedelics recklessly. This book is to provide information for a better understanding.

- Finally, contrary to one of my previous book's titles, psychedelics are not for everyone to take. Some people have pre-existing conditions or are prescribed medications that make psychedelic use unsafe. Please talk with a healthcare provider before engaging with psychedelics.

All that being said, it is time we have this conversation because we are seeing psychedelics everywhere- medical ketamine clinics and clinical trials, legalized psychedelics in the state of Oregon, and, soon, Colorado. Psychedelics have been decriminalized in a number of cities. There are even American psychedelic churches that are receiving federal exemptions to use psychedelics as sacraments as a part of their sincere religious practice.[2] After thousands of years of psychedelics being used for religious purposes, I love that the US government is finally giving the OK!

And I get it. During the last 50 years of prohibition we have heard so many lies about psychedelics that it is natural to have questions as to what to believe.

Did you know there are more than 200 academic institutions studying psychedelics? And while scientists don't know every aspect about exactly how psychedelics work in the mind and body, there is a general understanding that they often quiet down the part of your brain that is the inner narrator. This is the voice in your head that is constantly telling you to do more, produce more- that you are not worthy. Does that sound familiar?

It quiets that part down, and for me, that feels like the weight of the world is lifted off my shoulders.

Let's pause here for a moment. Take a moment to think about a time in your life when you felt stuck in the same routine, repeating the same thoughts or behaviors day after day. Like a record needle stuck in a groove? You are not alone- as we get older, we pair down our neural pathways and, biologically, we do get a bit "stuck in our ways." Some of us more than others.

It's like at some point, our minds went from running all over a playground to running on a treadmill, and no one told us. When we take a psychedelic, it often puts our minds back on the playground, and we remember that we are free to move all over this beautiful world. For our minds, this means we don't have to think about our relationships, or our jobs, or our lives the way we have been thinking about them. Psychedelics can help us break out of our repetitive thinking patterns and help us *remember*—remember that we have choices beyond the thought and behavioral patterns we are stuck in.

This breaking of repetitive thought patterns is why we are seeing psychedelics being studied for such a wide range of things, including substance use challenges,[3] OCD,[4] eating disorders,[5] and even autism.[6]

Let's go back to the "this is your brain and this is your brain on drugs" propaganda we were fed as kids. Remember the frying pan and the egg? When we actually look at brain images of our brain on psychedelics, what we see are lots of neural connections between areas of the brain that don't usually interact.[7] And, from the point of view of the participant, these new connections allow them to make new insights. This "lit up" brain is a visual representation of the insights and awarenesses that are happening while under the psychedelic.

Now, at this point you might be wondering, what about everything I learned about drugs leading to addiction and causing me great harm? Let's continue to explore that by looking at psilocybin as an example.

According to multiple studies, psilocybin is non-toxic and non-addictive.[8] There is a famous study from Dr. David Nutt at Imperial College London who compared various substances based on their harm to self and others.[9] Alcohol tops his list as the most dangerous, scoring a 72. Psilocybin mushrooms are at the opposite end of his scale, scoring a six.

I don't want to gloss over that "six" number. This doesn't mean that psilocybin is "safe", a lot of harm can happen in that six, and everyone considering taking psilocybin should be aware of this risk. Remember, all drugs have risks. Even acetaminophen, the active ingredient in some over-the-counter pain relievers, causes a few hundred deaths per year.[10] What we are talking about is *relative risk.*

Some keys to minimizing relative risk is understanding "Source" (where your psychedelics come from- real harm can be done from drugs being laced or contaminated), "Set" (the mindset of the participant- this speaks to the importance of preparation and to having strong support for after) and "Setting" (the physical environment- we are in quite a vulnerable position when in a non-ordinary state, it is important to really be in a safe place and around safe people). We are going to spend a lot of time discussing Set and Setting in this book.

One more important side note: psilocybin may be an FDA breakthrough therapy, but it remains classified as a Schedule 1 drug by the DEA, meaning in the US it is federally illegal outside of research.

Let's briefly look at another psychedelic, MDMA. You might have heard this called Molly or Ecstasy. MDMA is often referred to as a "heart opener" because it facilitates emotional breakthroughs by bringing suppressed memories, feelings, and traumas to the surface. It helps people view experiences without the weight of shame, blame, or guilt, allowing healing to begin. But again, MDMA is not a cure. It's a catalyst—it doesn't *do* the emotional work for you, it enables *you* to do it yourself.

To better understand the potential impact of MDMA, let's focus on veterans.

Did you know more than 17 US veterans commit suicide every day?[11]

Since 9/11, over 7,000 US service members have died during military operations, which is an awful amount of loss. In that same time period, over 30,000 US veterans and active duty personnel have taken their own lives.[12] This is more than four times the number lost in combat.

One reason is that conventional antidepressants, the kind prescribed most often, don't work for a lot of people who try them.[13] This is what science is trying to solve for. But here is some good news. There was a Phase-3 clinical trial focused on those treatment-resistant people using MDMA-assisted therapy. People where none of the existing treatment options worked.

After just three sessions of MDMA combined with therapy before and after, 71.2% of participants no longer met the criteria for PTSD.[14]

Let that sit in for a moment. Here are people- humans just like you and me and these people are suffering with PTSD and they have tried everything. Finally, something worked. This is remarkable.

And, it wasn't the medicine working by itself. The key here is that the therapeutic *process* was crucial to the success. This is why when submitting MDMA for regulatory approval, the drug developers bundled the therapy with the medicine. This is highly unusual in drug development.

Unfortunately, this phase-3 data didn't quite meet the FDA's requirements for approval just yet—they've asked for more data. But these results are incredibly promising for people like our veterans who are desperate for a new option.

What's also been encouraging is the rise of non-profit organizations stepping in to support veterans where the VA and our medical system falls short. Organizations like Heroic Hearts Project, VETS, and the Mission Within are helping to send veterans to places like Central and South America—and now Oregon—where they can legally access psychedelics.

I had the privilege to spend a week in Peru with Heroic Hearts Project and a group of veterans working with Ayahuasca under the guidance of Shipibo healers, and I witnessed and experienced the profound impact these sacred ceremonies can have. I have also seen how veterans use group and individual integration sessions to transform the newfound insights and awarenesses that they discover during ceremonies into real, meaningful lasting change.

The integration process amplifies the benefits of the insights and awarenesses brought on by the medicine. It is also the place where we have the time to process and unpack what came up during our psychedelic experiences. For some people, the integration process takes months or even years. This book has a number of integration exercises for you to try.

Again, psychedelics are powerful catalysts, not cures.

Let's look at one more group that may be profoundly impacted by psychedelics—those facing end-of-life distress. For people confronting end-of-life, they know psychedelics won't change the outcome, but they hope it can transform the quality of the time they have left.

Pause here and take a moment to imagine you were given a terminal diagnosis. It would be understandable for you to feel depressed, anxious, scared, hopeless. Now, during this period, would you like to take a few months to try out an antidepressant to see if it helps? And then, if it doesn't, ween yourself off and try again?

A study at New York University found that a single dose of psilocybin offered rapid and profound relief from depression, anxiety, and hopelessness in cancer patients, with an 83% response rate.[15]

But what's even more incredible? In a follow-up study, about 80% of the patients still alive reported that the positive effects had lasted for 4½ years.[16] This means that a single psychedelic session provided long-term emotional and psychological benefits.

Many participants reported a completely new understanding of life and death. Instead of fear, they were able to confront their mortality with acceptance. I believe it was this shift in perspective, brought on by the psychedelic but assigned meaning by the participant, that helped alleviate their suffering.

Now let's make this even more interesting. In the spiritual or ceremonial practices with psychedelics, sometimes psychedelics aren't just given to the person who is dying, but also to their friends and family. Can you imagine how transformative it must be for everyone involved to share in this healing process? Can you imagine the conversations that unfold, the emotional breakthroughs that happen, and the peace that's found?

The medical world is also thinking about this. There's now a phase 2 study exploring just this very idea- not just treating the cancer patient but including one significant other.[17]

Over and over we are seeing research that says that this medicine is powerful but not just because of a bio-chemical reaction, but because of the journey it takes the patients on. The "trip" if you will. Sometimes these journeys are beautiful, and sometimes these journeys are challenging.

Let's do one more exercise. Can you think to yourself of anything in your life that you carried (or still carry) that felt too heavy to share with anyone? Maybe you tried to move on, pretending it never happened, but deep down, you knew it did?

For me, this moment came during puberty, involving an extended family member. It was something I had buried for over 25 years. And then, during a psychedelic experience, that memory resurfaced and I was able to see the experience differently.

One of the things we are taught when working with psychedelics is that when we have challenging experiences, not to resist them. What you resist, persists. If you see a dragon, we are told that rather than running away, crawl up through its nose and look out its eyes.

When this memory surfaced, I did as I was taught, and suddenly I was able to see her not through the lens of my pain and shame but through hers. Without condoning her actions, I could understand her loneliness, her sadness. Without condoning her actions, I could see her not as a person to fear, but as someone deeply wounded. And then my own healing began. Through this newfound empathy, I could finally release years of shame, blame, and guilt, and I found peace.

And this is the promise of psychedelics—They don't rewrite the story for us magically. They enable us to rewrite our own stories.

Psychedelics don't help us avoid or numb the pain; they help us discover it, understand it, and transform it.

And this process is why, with psychedelics, in many ways, you are the medicine.

Psychedelics can't rewrite the past or bring back those we've lost, but they can help us find deeper meaning in the present.

Psychedelics are catalysts, not cures.

With love-

Matt Zemon
Chapel Hill, NC

This introduction was adapted from a TEDx talk originally delivered in Johannesburg, South Africa. It has been expanded and edited for clarity to fit the context of this book.

References:

1. Griffiths, R. R., M. W. Johnson, W. A. Richards, B. D. Richards, U. McCann, and R. Jesse. 2011. "Psilocybin occasioned mystical-type experiences: immediate and persisting dose-related effects." *Psychopharmacology (Berl)* 218 (4): 649-65. https://doi.org/10.1007/s00213-011-2358-5.

2. Church of the Eagle and the Condor et al. v. Garland et al., 22-cv-01004-SRB (D. Ariz.). (2024). Settlement Agreement and Release. https://psychedelicalpha.com/wp-content/uploads/2024/05/6-CEC-Agreement-24-4-12-signed.pdf

3. Yaden DB, Berghella AP, Regier PS, Garcia-Romeu A, Johnson MW, Hendricks PS. Classic psychedelics in the treatment of substance use disorder: Potential synergies with twelve-step programs. Int J Drug Policy. 2021 Dec;98:103380. doi: 10.1016/j.drugpo.2021.103380. Epub 2021 Jul 27. PMID: 34329952.

4. Graziosi, M., Rohde, J. S., Tiwari, P., Siev, J., & Yaden, D. B. (2024). Psychedelics, OCD and related disorders: A systematic review. Journal of Obsessive-Compulsive and Related Disorders, 41, 100873. https://doi.org/https://doi.org/10.1016/j.jocrd.2024.100873

5. Spriggs, M. J., Kettner, H., & Carhart-Harris, R. L. (2021). Positive effects of psychedelics on depression and wellbeing scores in individuals reporting an eating disorder. Eating and Weight Disorders - Studies on Anorexia, Bulimia and Obesity, 26(4), 1265-1270. https://doi.org/10.1007/s40519-020-01000-8

6. Markopoulos, A., Inserra, A., De Gregorio, D., & Gobbi, G. (2022). Evaluating the Potential Use of Serotonergic Psychedelics in Autism Spectrum Disorder. Frontiers in pharmacology, 12, 749068. https://doi.org/10.3389/fphar.2021.749068

7. Carhart-Harris, R. L., Erritzoe, D., Williams, T., Stone, J. M., Reed, L. J., Colasanti, A., Tyacke, R. J., Leech, R., Malizia, A. L., Murphy, K., Hobden, P., Evans, J., Feilding, A., Wise, R. G., & Nutt, D. J. (2012). Neural correlates of the psychedelic state as determined by fMRI studies with psilocybin. Proc Natl Acad Sci U S A, 109(6), 2138-2143. https://doi.org/10.1073/pnas.1119598109

8. Nichols, D. E. (2004). Hallucinogens. Pharmacology & therapeutics, 101(2), 131-181. https://maps.org/research-archive/w3pb/2004/2004_Nichols_22684_1.pdf

9. Nutt, D., King, L., & Phillips, L. (2010). Drug harms in the UK: A multi-criterion decision analysis. Lancet, 376. https://bigfatgenius.com/2220%20Fall%202010/Nutt%20King%20Phillips%20-%20Drug%20Harms%20in%20the%20UK.pdf

10. Nourjah, P., Ahmad, S. R., Karwoski, C., & Willy, M. (2006). Estimates of acetaminophen (Paracetomal)-associated overdoses in the United States. Pharmacoepidemiology and drug safety, 15(6), 398-405. https://onlinelibrary.wiley.com/doi/10.1002/pds.1191

11. Affairs, U. D. o. V. (2023). National veteran suicide prevention annual report. Edited by Office of Mental Health and Suicide Prevention. https://www.mentalhealth.va.gov/docs/data-sheets/2023/2023-National-Veteran-Suicide-Prevention-Annual-Report-FINAL-508.pdf

12. Suitt, T. H. (2021). High suicide rates among United States service members and veterans of the post-9/11 wars. Costs of War Project. https://watson.brown.edu/costsofwar/files/cow/imce/papers/2021/Suitt_Suicides_Costs%20of%20War_June%2021%202021.pdf

13. Yuan, Ziqi, Zhenlei Chen, Maoqiang Xue, Jie Zhang, and Lige Leng. 2020. "Application of antidepressants in depression: A systematic review and meta-analysis." Journal of Clinical Neuroscience 80: 169-181. https://doi.org/10.1016/j.jocn.2020.08.013

14. Mitchell, J. M., Ot'alora G, M., van der Kolk, B., Shannon, S., Bogenschutz, M., Gelfand, Y., Paleos, C., Nicholas, C. R., Quevedo, S., Balliett, B., Hamilton, S., Mithoefer, M., Kleiman, S., Parker-Guilbert, K., Tzarfaty, K., Harrison, C., de Boer, A., Doblin, R., Yazar-Klosinski, B., & Group, M. S. C. (2023). MDMA-assisted therapy for moderate to severe PTSD: a randomized, placebo-controlled phase 3 trial. Nature Medicine, 29(10), 2473-2480. https://doi.org/10.1038/s41591-023-02565-4

15. Ross, S., Bossis, A., Guss, J., Agin-Liebes, G., Malone, T., Cohen, B., Mennenga, S. E., Belser, A., Kalliontzi, K., Babb, J., Su, Z., Corby, P., & Schmidt, B. L. (2016). Rapid and sustained symptom reduction following psilocybin treatment for anxiety and depression in patients with life-threatening cancer: a randomized controlled trial. Journal of psychopharmacology (Oxford), 30(12), 1165-1180. https://doi.org/10.1177/0269881116675512

16. Agin-Liebes, G. I., Malone, T., Yalch, M. M., Mennenga, S. E., Ponté, K. L., Guss, J., Bossis, A. P., Grigsby, J., Fischer, S., & Ross, S. (2020). Long-term follow-up of psilocybin-assisted psychotherapy for psychiatric and existential distress in patients with life-threatening cancer. Journal of Psychopharmacology, 34(2), 155-166. https://doi.org/10.1177/0269881119897615

17. MDMA-assisted Therapy for Adjustment Disorder (AD) in Dyads of Patients With Cancer and a Concerned Significant Other https://clinicaltrials.gov/study/NCT05584826?term=sunstone%20therapies&intr=%20&rank=5

HOW TO USE THIS WORKBOOK

This workbook is designed to guide you from the preparatory stages of your journey through the integration that follows your experience. It offers opportunities for deep engagement, from basic exercises to thought-provoking prompts, all facilitating personal growth and healing.

Essentials for the New Explorer

In easy-to-understand language, this section explains background information to make an informed decision about participating in a psychedelic experience. Topics include:

- Types and effects of psychedelic substances.
- Types of settings for psychedelic work, including ceremonies, retreats, and therapy.
- Significance of setting intentions.
- Creating an optimal setting for your journey.
- Best practices for integration.
- Guidance for facing potential challenges.

By providing this overview, in addition to resources and support networks, this guide aims to empower you with a foundation for an informed and transformative psychedelic journey. That being said, every experience is unique, and you may receive specific instructions from your facilitator that you will need to follow.

Preparation

The preparation phase is essential in setting the stage for a safe and insightful psychedelic experience. This section is designed to equip you with tools and exercises that enhance your readiness—mentally, physically, and spiritually. By engaging deeply with these preparatory activities, you prime yourself for a transformative journey, ensuring you are well-prepared to navigate the profound and often intense experiences that psychedelics can induce.

- **Mental and Spiritual Preparation:** Here, you'll find exercises aimed at aligning your mind and spirit with the intentions of your journey. These include meditation practices and intention-setting exercises that help clarify your goals and prepare your psyche for the transformative potential of psychedelics.

- **Physical Preparation:** This part provides guidelines on how to prepare your body for the journey. It covers dietary recommendations, known as 'dieta,' and physical health tips to ensure your body is in optimal condition to handle the physical effects of psychedelics.

- **Homelife and Relationship Preparation:** Prepare your living environment and relationships for your return post-experience. This includes advice on setting supportive spaces at home and communicating with loved ones about what to expect.

- **Reflective Journaling Exercises:** These deepen your self-awareness and help you articulate your thoughts, feelings, and expectations about the journey.

- **Discovering Your Intention Exercises:** Helps you pinpoint the purpose of your journey, enhancing the focus and direction of your psychedelic experience.

- **Identifying Your Support Exercises:** Outlines how to establish a support system, crucial for both pre-journey preparations and post-journey integration.

- **Meditation Exercises:** Offers a variety of meditation techniques to cultivate mindfulness, reduce pre-journey anxiety, and increase mental clarity.

- **Grounding Exercises:** These exercises are designed to help you connect with the present moment and stabilize your emotions before and after your psychedelic journey.

- **Packing Essentials for a Psychedelic Retreat:** Lists critical items that can comfort and aid your journey, ensuring you're well-equipped.

Through these exercises and checklists, this workbook provides a structured approach to preparing for a psychedelic journey, addressing all facets of readiness. By completing these steps, you ensure that you are not just physically prepared but also mentally and emotionally primed for the experiences and insights that await.

The Journey

Adaptable to your unique journey, the Journey Logs included in this workbook offer a framework for creating a record of your thoughts, feelings, visions, and revelations during each stage of your psychedelic exploration.

Integration

The days and weeks following your psychedelic experience are rich with changes in your daily life. In this section you will find weekly themed exercises to help you identify and process these developments.

- **Week 1: "Embracing Change and Cultivating New Habits":** Start by identifying and letting go of outdated patterns, beliefs, or emotions to clear the path for personal transformation. Engage in exercises designed not only to facilitate this release but also to initiate the formation of new, positive habits that align with your authentic self and support lasting change.

- **Week 2: "New Sensations":** Engage in activities designed to open you up to fresh sensations, ideas, and perspectives. This week is about embracing the newness that comes from your journey and exploring the expanded boundaries of your experience.

- **Week 3: "Revisiting The Past":** Take a deeper dive into your past, revisiting previous experiences with a new lens. This week's exercises encourage a compassionate reflection on your life's path and the lessons learned along the way.

- **Week 4: "Envisioning the Future":** Using the insights gained from your journey, start envisioning your path forward. Engage in exercises that help you outline actionable steps toward realizing your future aspirations.

Daily: Commit to daily practices of gratitude and journaling to recognize and celebrate the transformative experiences you've undergone. These practices serve as a foundation for sustained growth and self-discovery.

As Desired: Engage in Creative Play whenever you feel the urge for an escape or a moment of mindfulness. These activities are designed to stimulate your imagination, provide relief, and express yourself joyfully.

People encounter psychedelics within both therapeutic and ceremonial contexts, and this book is designed to be versatile across both medical and spiritual environments. Recognizing the diverse settings in which healing can occur, the language throughout the book may interchangeably refer to therapeutic, ceremonial, or coaching scenarios. This flexibility ensures that the guide remains a valuable tool in supporting you through your transformative journeys, whether in a clinical setting or a more spiritual context.

After completing this book, we humbly recommend Beyond The Trip for future journeys. Beyond The Trip contains all the activities found within this book without the additional surrounding content.

Therapists and Coaches: For therapists and coaches supporting people using this workbook, we invite you to order our **coaches and therapists edition**, co-written by Ken Weingardt, PhD and designed to enhance the workbook's content. You can also order discounted bulk copies of this workbook here:

www.mattzemon.com/beginners

ESSENTIALS FOR THE NEW EXPLORER

"Be smarter every day by listening to your intuition, looking at the world with your forehead. Jump, dance, sing, so that you live happier. Heal yourself, with beautiful love and always remember...You are the medicine."

-Maria Sabina
Mazatec curandera

Essentials for the New Explorer

This section of the workbook serves as your entry point to the psychedelic experience, providing you with the knowledge needed to participate thoughtfully and informedly. Within these pages, you will learn some basics about psychedelics, uncovering their history, the nuances of their effects, and the current legal framework governing their use.

Moreover, this section offers an overview of the psychedelics shown to facilitate healing and growth. The aim here is to guide you in approaching this exploration with the care, respect, and informed perspective it demands. By engaging with this section, you'll be better positioned to determine if a psychedelic journey resonates with your needs for healing and spiritual growth.

INTRODUCTION TO PSYCHEDELICS

Psychedelics are a category of potent substances that can alter perceptions, emotions, and cognitive processes. Common examples include psilocybin (found in magic mushrooms), DMT, ayahuasca, ibogaine, ketamine, MDA/MDMA, and mescaline (derived from cacti like Peyote and San Pedro).

A Historical Perspective

The term "psychedelic" was coined in the 1950s by British psychiatrist Humphrey Osmond and means, "mind manifesting". Indigenous peoples worldwide have utilized psychedelics in spiritual and healing rituals for thousands of years, including ayahuasca ceremonies in South America, iboga and mushroom rituals in Africa, mushroom ceremonies in Siberia, and peyote ceremonies among Native Americans, just to name a few. Currently, we're experiencing a "psychedelic renaissance," with renewed interest in their potential for treating mental health issues, supported by research at over 200 academic institutions globally.

Legality

Ketamine stands out as the only psychedelic drug that's legally allowed across the US for therapy. This is a big change from the rules set in the 1970s, which made most psychedelics illegal. The reasons behind those old rules were more about politics than health. John Ehrlichman, who worked with President Nixon, said that the government's fight against drugs was really a way to target Nixon's political opponents and African Americans by linking them to drug use and crime. This led to a lot of wrong ideas about psychedelics and made it harder for people to see how some drugs could actually help in therapy.

Today there is a shift happening in places like Oregon and Colorado, where people voted to allow adults to use psychedelics for therapy. This doesn't mean psychedelics are totally legal, but it's a step toward understanding their benefits and focusing on health rather than punishment.

Cities across the US are making similar changes, and new laws are being proposed that could change things even more. Around the world, some countries are more open to providing access to psychedelics. For example, in Costa Rica, Ayahuasca and Ibogaine are not restricted, and other psychedelics are decriminalized. Canada and Australia are making it easier for people to get treatment with psychedelics like psilocybin and MDMA. In Jamaica, it's legal to grow and sell psilocybin mushrooms. Mexico allows certain psychedelics for spiritual reasons, and Peru legally allows Ayahuasca and San Pedro.

In the US, religious freedom is protected by the First Amendment and the Religious Freedom Restoration Act. But, while the ability to use psychedelics in ceremonial settings may be protected by law and statute, only a few spiritual groups have clear legal permission to use psychedelics in their ceremonies. This area of the law is complex, and people need to be careful and informed if they're using psychedelics as part of their religion.

Psychedelic Experiences Vary

Psychedelic drugs can lead to many different kinds of experiences, from deep personal insights to feeling a strong connection with the world. What happens during these experiences depends on the psychedelic you take, how much you take, and where you are mentally and physically when you take it. You might feel strong emotions, see things differently, or think in new ways.

Sometimes, taking psychedelics can make your heart beat faster, your blood pressure go up or down, and your body temperature change. Some people might feel sick to their stomach, especially with drugs like ayahuasca, ibogaine, and sometimes mushrooms.

The amount of the medicine you take, called the "dosage," really affects your experience. A small change in the amount can make a big difference in what you feel. Your "set," which is how you're feeling inside, and your "setting," or where you are when you take the drug, also play a big part.

At higher doses, psychedelics can make you feel a deep connection to everything, like you're part of a bigger universe, or give you insights into deep questions. People often feel more connected to nature and others, leading to a strong sense of empathy.

But, taking psychedelics can also bring up tough emotions or past traumas. That's why having someone with you who knows about how the medicines work can be very helpful. They can help you stay calm and feel safe, which can make a big difference in how your journey goes.

Because psychedelic experiences can vary and be intense, being prepared in a comfortable and risk-reduced setting is key to a positive and safe experience. Learning about each psychedelic, how to get ready, and creating a supportive environment are important steps for healing and growing. Remember, the amount you take, how you're feeling, and where you are (your dosage, set, and setting) are the foundations of a successful psychedelic experience.

Psychedelics can also make things worse. While this doesn't happen often, there have been people who have experienced various levels of impairment following a psychedelic experience. Knowing this is possible is part of making a responsible decision on whether working with psychedelics is right for you.

HOW THEY WORK

The therapeutic benefits of psychedelics are thought to arise from their ability to produce profound shifts in consciousness and perception, leading to increased neuroplasticity—the brain's capacity to reorganize itself by forming new neural connections. This process is pivotal for breaking habitual patterns of thinking and behavior. Psychedelics promote the formation of new connections by activating neurons that may not have communicated in years, fostering novel thought patterns and perspectives. This enhanced brain connectivity helps individuals to overcome deeply ingrained psychological barriers, leading to substantial and enduring improvements in mental health and cognitive functions.

In addition, psychedelics disrupt the default mode network (DMN), a brain network associated with introspective thoughts and the maintenance of one's sense of ego. The modulation of the DMN can reduce symptoms in various psychological conditions, including depression and anxiety, by helping individuals gain new perspectives on their life situations. This contributes to lasting improvements in mood and overall mental outlook.

Many participants in psychedelic research report experiencing mystical states that include feelings of unity, transcendence beyond time and space, and profound joy. These experiences often facilitate a connection to something greater than oneself, described as deeply sacred or spiritual.

PTSD AND PSYCHEDELICS

Post-traumatic Stress Disorder (PTSD) is a serious challenge faced by many individuals, often arising from a wide range of traumatic experiences. While commonly associated with veterans and victims of sexual assault, PTSD can affect anyone who has encountered significant trauma. This condition often persists long after the initial event and can be further complicated by physical injuries or other life circumstances.

The Impact of PTSD

Living with PTSD can feel like being trapped in a perpetual cycle of past trauma, where moments of fear, pain, and danger replay uncontrollably in your mind. It's not just about battling vivid nightmares or flashbacks; it's the constant state of alertness, the unexpected surges of paranoia, and the struggle with feelings of detachment from those around you. This condition doesn't just revisit you during moments of quiet but invades every aspect of your daily life, making simple tasks feel insurmountable and isolating you within your own experiences of suffering.

Many individuals with PTSD may minimize their suffering, believing others have it worse and questioning their right to seek help. This mindset can lead to a muted existence, where happiness seems unattainable. It's vital to understand that pain is not comparative to others; your experiences are valid, and you deserve support.

Healing Through Psychedelics

The path to overcoming PTSD is deeply personal, and traditional therapies may not be effective for everyone. Psychedelic-assisted treatment offers a new avenue for healing, with substances like ayahuasca, psilocybin, and MDMA facilitating emotional breakthroughs and reconnection with lost parts of the self. Remarkably, two recent studies found that over 70%-80% of the people with PTSD who tried a program using psychedelics and therapy saw significant improvements and no longer fit the diagnosis for PTSD, typically without significant side effects. This evidence underscores the promise these treatments hold, offering substantial improvements in symptoms for many who had previously seen little hope for recovery.

Psychedelics aren't a one-size-fits-all solution, but they represent a potent option for those battling PTSD and other challenges. The key message for anyone living with PTSD is that your suffering is acknowledged, your journey towards healing is supported, and peace is within reach. You're not meant to walk this path alone, and the evolving landscape of psychedelic-assisted treatment ensures you don't have to.

What to know about PTSD

PTSD can stem from any traumatic event, not just war or sexual assault. Its impact is profound, leading to a range of symptoms that can disrupt daily life and exacerbate feelings of isolation. However, it's important to remember that PTSD is a treatable condition, not a life sentence. Community support, innovative treatments like psychedelics, and a growing awareness of PTSD's effects are all part of a changing landscape that offers hope and pathways to healing.

- Where there is war, there is PTSD.

- While PTSD is commonly associated with the aftermath of war, it can result from any traumatic event.

- The effects of PTSD can include sudden, unexpected attacks of paranoia, flashbacks, depression, hopelessness, suicidal thinking, insomnia, hypervigilance, headaches, social isolation, and other kinds of suffering.

- Substance use can provide temporary relief but often worsens PTSD symptoms in the long run.

- PTSD can inadvertently be passed along to spouses, family, and other loved ones, who may experience depression, anxiety, hopelessness, fatigue, and more as a result.

- PTSD is not a matter of poor character, weakness, cowardice, or insanity. It is a legitimate health condition with serious implications for a person's physical and mental well-being.

- If you have PTSD, you are not alone.

- Traditional treatment programs for PTSD have low rates of completion and success.

PSYCHEDELICS FOR DEPRESSION AND ANXIETY

Psychedelics are increasingly viewed as a significant breakthrough in the treatment of depression and anxiety. This perspective is bolstered by numerous studies indicating that substances such as psilocybin, ayahuasca, MDMA, and LSD can provide substantial relief where traditional medications may fall short.

Effectiveness in Treating Depression

Recent studies show that psychedelics can quickly reduce symptoms of depression in a way that traditional antidepressants often cannot. Unlike traditional antidepressants, which often take weeks to take effect and may not work for everyone, psychedelics can produce noticeable improvements in symptoms within hours after a single dose. These effects can last from several weeks to years, providing substantial relief for individuals who have struggled with persistent depression

Psilocybin, for instance, has demonstrated potential not only in easing standard depressive symptoms but also in addressing treatment-resistant forms of depression. Research suggests that a single dose can bring about rapid, significant, and lasting improvements. A notable study from Johns Hopkins University highlighted that a significant portion of participants achieved lasting symptom relief for many months following just two psilocybin sessions.

Ayahuasca, a psychedelic brew traditionally used by indigenous tribes in the Amazon, has also gained recognition in the scientific community for its potential to treat depression and anxiety. A randomized, placebo-controlled clinical trial conducted in Brazil demonstrated that a single session of ayahuasca could lead to significant improvements in symptoms of depression and anxiety that are sustained over time. Participants reported experiencing profound introspective insights and a sense of spiritual enlightenment that contributed to their emotional healing.

Anxiety Reduction

Similarly, psychedelics have shown promise in treating various forms of anxiety. Psychedelics help alleviate the existential distress and anxiety that often accompany severe illnesses. Studies have reported that psychedelic-assisted therapy can lead to significant reductions in both anxiety and depression, which are sustained over extended periods post-treatment.

The potential of psychedelics to alleviate anxiety is garnering significant attention as well due to the limitations of traditional pharmacological and talk therapy treatments, which often fall short in terms of effectiveness and side effects. Recent reviews and clinical trials highlight psychedelics' ability to bring about rapid and sustained reductions in anxiety symptoms across various disorders, showcasing a promising alternative for those resistant to standard therapies.

Studies incorporating substances like psilocybin, MDMA, and ayahuasca have shown that a single therapeutic session can lead to immediate and long-lasting improvements in anxiety levels, significantly enhancing quality of life and social functioning. This effectiveness is attributed to psychedelics' unique capacity to induce profound shifts in consciousness, allowing individuals to reinterpret and integrate emotional and cognitive processes related to anxiety. Unlike traditional treatments that may require continuous dosing and often come with undesirable side effects, psychedelics offer a therapeutic breakthrough after just one or a few sessions, often without severe adverse reactions.

Moreover, the safety profile of these substances, when administered in controlled settings, has been consistently validated, showing that they are well-tolerated and have a low risk for addiction compared to traditional medications. The experiences reported by patients—ranging from profound existential insights to feelings of interconnectedness and peace—highlight the dual therapeutic and transformative potential of psychedelics.

ADDICTION AND PSYCHEDELICS

The use of psychedelics to treat addiction may seem counterintuitive, as traditionally, recovery models emphasize abstinence from all psychoactive substances. However, a growing body of research suggests that psychedelics, largely non-addictive in nature, can offer significant benefits in breaking the cycle of addiction. Unlike many addictive substances that compel continuous use to avoid withdrawal symptoms, psychedelics such as psilocybin do not generally lead to dependence or compulsive use.

One notable figure in the history of psychedelics and addiction treatment is Bill Wilson, the co-founder of Alcoholics Anonymous (AA). Wilson himself explored the potential of LSD in the late 1950s and early 1960s as a tool to facilitate profound spiritual experiences that could lead to recovery from alcoholism.

He theorized that LSD could help hardened alcoholics achieve a "spiritual awakening," thus enabling them to see life from a different perspective and potentially break the cycle of addiction. This idea was controversial within AA and remains a topic of debate in recovery communities.

Wilson's theory highlighted a broader hypothesis that has gained traction in recent years: psychedelics might help address the root psychological triggers of addiction by promoting enhanced self-awareness and emotional insights. Modern studies have explored this hypothesis further. Research at institutions like Johns Hopkins University and New York University has investigated psilocybin-assisted therapy as a treatment for nicotine addiction and alcohol dependence, respectively, with promising results. These studies indicate that psilocybin, often in just a single session combined with psychotherapy, can significantly reduce cravings and relapse rates.

The mechanism behind this therapeutic effect may involve the ability of psychedelics to disrupt maladaptive neural patterns—like those associated with addiction—allowing the brain to reset its behavior around substance use. Following the psychedelic experience itself, psychedelics foster a temporary state of heightened neuroplasticity, which can help individuals adjust their behaviors and reprogram their beliefs about themselves and their addiction.

In addition to psilocybin, studies with ibogaine are showing promise for their use with opioid disorders.

Looking forward, the challenge will be to integrate psychedelic therapies into mainstream addiction treatment in a way that is both ethically and medically sound. This paradigm shift in the treatment of addiction represents not just a medical advancement but also a broader cultural shift towards understanding and treating substance use disorders in a more holistic and compassionate manner. It is important to also note that ketamine, which is legal for doctors to use in the US, poses a higher risk of addiction than other psychedelics. While medical use of ketamine under strict supervision has not shown significant issues with dependency, recreational or unsupervised use can lead to health complications and dependency, as individuals might increase their dosage to keep the effects of the ketamine high.

TYPES OF SETTINGS FOR PSYCHEDELIC WORK

Psychedelic experiences can vary greatly depending on the setting in which they take place. Understanding these different environments can help you choose the one that best suits your needs and goals. Selecting the appropriate setting depends on your personal preferences, the nature of the issues you wish to address, and your comfort level with different environments. Each setting offers unique benefits and challenges, so consider your needs and discuss options with a trusted therapist or guide.

Psychedelic Assisted Therapy

Psychedelic-assisted therapy involves the use of specific psychedelic substances in a clinical setting under the supervision of medical professionals. These substances, including ketamine, MDMA, ibogaine, and psilocybin, are used to enhance therapeutic processes and facilitate profound emotional and psychological healing. This setting offers a highly controlled and safe environment, ensuring medical oversight and integrating both medical and psychological care. Studies have shown that this is particularly effective for treating conditions like PTSD, depression, anxiety, and substance use challenges.

Healing Ceremonies

Healing ceremonies involve the use of traditional plant medicines such as ayahuasca, psilocybin mushrooms, mescaline, and iboga in a ritualistic and often communal setting. Sometimes these ceremonies also include synthetic medicines like MDMA, Sassafras (MDA), and 5-MeO-DMT. These ceremonies are typically led by experienced shaman, taitas, maestros, curanderos, or "guides" who lead participants through the experience with specific rituals and practices. The setting is usually natural and serene, providing a sacred space for deep spiritual and emotional healing. This environment emphasizes a connection to nature and the collective experience of the group and does not make medical claims.

International Retreats

Psychedelic retreats are structured programs, often (but not always) held in countries where the medicines are legal or decriminalized, designed to provide a comprehensive and immersive experience. These retreats typically include multiple sessions, integration support, and a community of participants. The setting is controlled, risk-reduced, and typically staffed by experienced facilitators who guide the sessions. Retreats can be medically based, ceremonially based, or a hybrid of the two.

Individual Practitioners

Some individuals may choose to work with individual practitioners who offer psychedelic experiences outside of formal or legal frameworks.

These practitioners often have significant experience and knowledge but operate without formal regulation. **It's crucial to thoroughly vet any individual practitioners for safety, ethics, and competence.** (See the section on "Finding a Quality Psychedelic Experience" later in this workbook.) This setting requires a high degree of trust and personal responsibility.

INDIVIDUAL VS GROUP

After deciding what type of setting you wish to participate in, the next question is whether you would prefer it to be conducted individually or in a group.

Individual Sessions

Individual sessions offer a one-on-one (or one-on-two) experience with a trained therapist or guide. This setting allows for highly personalized attention and support, tailored to your specific needs and goals. The therapist or guide can help navigate the experience in real-time, providing immediate interventions and insights. **For maximum safety and support, current best practices recommend having two facilitators present**. This ensures that personal care and safety are maintained throughout the session. This setting is ideal for those seeking deep, focused, and private work on personal issues.

Some ketamine providers are offering at-home sessions with ketamine. For those with experience and confidence in managing their psychedelic experiences, at-home sessions offer flexibility and comfort. It's crucial to prepare thoroughly, ensuring you have a trusted sitter present and creating a safe, calming environment. While more convenient, this setting requires significant self-responsibility and understanding of the substances used. We do not recommend this for anyone experiencing significant depression, PTSD, or active suicidality.

Group Sessions

Group sessions involve several participants experiencing psychedelics together, usually guided by one or more facilitators. This setting fosters a sense of community and shared experience, allowing participants to support each other. Group dynamics can enhance the therapeutic or ceremonial process by providing different perspectives and shared insights. However, it's essential to feel comfortable with the group to benefit fully from this setting.

Conclusion

By understanding the various settings for psychedelic work, you can make an informed decision that aligns with your goals, ensuring a supportive and enriching experience.

As we continue to navigate the complexities of mental health treatment, psychedelics offer a promising alternative to traditional therapies, particularly for conditions that are resistant to conventional methods. The inclusion of substances such as MDMA, psilocybin, ayahuasca, and ibogaine in our therapeutic toolkit not only broadens our understanding of mental wellness but also deepens our respect for both ancient traditions and modern science. As research progresses and legal frameworks evolve, the potential of these substances to significantly impact both public health and personal well-being becomes increasingly apparent.

COMMON PSYCHEDELICS

Ayahuasca

Ayahuasca, known as the "vine of the soul," plays a significant role in the spiritual and healing traditions of many indigenous tribes in the Amazon. This powerful brew, made from the ayahuasca vine and chacruna leaves, is famous for its ability to create deep, transformative experiences. People who drink ayahuasca might see vivid visions, hear sounds more intensely, and feel a deep connection to the world around them in ways that can change their lives.

The journey with ayahuasca isn't just about these mind-opening experiences; it's also a path to emotional and spiritual discovery. Its reach has expanded globally, attracting individuals seeking its profound effects under the guidance of both indigenous shamans and modern practitioners. Although research supports its quick-acting antidepressant qualities and overall safety when used responsibly, more studies are needed to fully unlock its therapeutic potential.

The unique impact of ayahuasca comes from the special mix of its ingredients. The vine contains substances that allow DMT in the chacruna leaves to be effective when taken by mouth. The experience is highly personal, shaped by the specific makeup of the brew, the environment, and the participant's mental and physical state.

During an ayahuasca ceremony, participants might feel like they're stepping out of everyday reality, encountering spiritual beings, or looking at past experiences from a new angle. Even individuals with PTSD have reported significant benefits, although there's caution advised due to the potential for re-traumatization.

Physically, the experience might include nausea and vomiting, often seen as part of the healing process. Emotionally and spiritually, ayahuasca can open up a range of states, from blissful unity with everything to confronting inner demons, demanding resilience, and offering deep insights in return.

Preparing for an ayahuasca ceremony is essential. Traditions and medical best practices suggest following specific dietary and behavioral guidelines to ensure a safe and impactful experience. This includes avoiding particular foods, substances, and certain medications, especially SSRIs, to prevent harmful interactions.

While ayahuasca holds the potential for deep healing, it's not recommended for everyone, especially those with certain mental health conditions or histories of psychosis. Please make sure you have a medical clearance before using this psychedelic. Its legal status also varies, with ayahuasca being illegal in many places due to its DMT content, though some religious groups in the U.S. have secured legal exemptions.

The potential for personal transformation with ayahuasca is significant. However, it's important to approach it with caution, thorough preparation, and professional guidance, recognizing the risks involved. Fatalities related to its use usually stem from unsafe practices or interactions with other medications, not from ayahuasca itself. This highlights the importance of a safe setting and careful health consideration for anyone thinking about participating in an ayahuasca ceremony.

Ibogaine

Ibogaine, a powerful substance found in the iboga shrub from Africa, is catching the eye of many for its ability to help with challenging problems like opioid addiction and even Parkinson's disease. Yet, its strong and long-lasting effects, which can lead to serious and sometimes deadly side effects, make it a topic of debate and caution.

The rules around ibogaine are complex. In the U.S. it is illegal and labeled as a Schedule 1 narcotic, but in other places like Brazil, New Zealand, and South Africa, doctors can prescribe it. The iboga shrub is now protected in Gabon to prevent it from being overharvested, showing the challenges of using it responsibly and ethically.

If someone is considering ibogaine treatment, they need to find a clinic that understands the risks and has the right people to guide them safely. Despite not being closely regulated, the patient is responsible for making sure they're making a safe choice.

Ibogaine works differently from other psychedelics, affecting various parts of the brain and showing promise in stopping addiction. However, its effect on the heart's rhythm is risky, so a thorough heart check, like an EKG, and medical exam is a must to avoid life-threatening problems. This careful approach is essential for anyone thinking about this path.

The use of natural iboga in spiritual practices like Bwiti rituals adds another layer to its significance, raising questions about how it's used today. With the iboga plant becoming harder to find, some clinics are looking into more sustainable options, such as the Voacanga africana plant.

Ibogaine holds promise, especially for those struggling with opioid addiction, offering a glimmer of hope in the fight against the opioid crisis. But, it's essential to weigh the benefits against the risks and ethical issues involved.

Getting ready for an ibogaine experience means preparing both medically and spiritually, underlining the need for expert guidance to handle the powerful experiences it can bring.

Choosing the right ibogaine treatment center means putting safety first, with thorough health checks and emergency plans. It's important to go with centers known for their ethical approach and commitment to patient safety.

While ibogaine offers an intriguing option for treating addiction and exploring spirituality, it demands careful thought about its legality, risks, and the ethics of its use. Being one of the psychedelics with higher physical risks, it's crucial for those interested to proceed with caution, armed with the right information and support from seasoned professionals.

Ketamine

Ketamine became famous for its use as an anesthetic on the battlefields of the Vietnam War and has come a long way since. It's now seen as a groundbreaking treatment for challenging cases of depression, PTSD, and chronic pain, especially for those who haven't found help from standard treatments. Approved by the FDA in 1970, ketamine's journey from the operating room to the psychiatrist's office highlights its unique properties, including its ability to keep heart and blood pressure stable during medical procedures.

What sets ketamine apart in the mental health field is its fast-acting relief for depression and PTSD symptoms, offering hope to those in urgent need. As the only psychedelic treatment that's legally available in the United States for such conditions, its role in therapy is growing.

Ketamine works in complex ways, interacting with different parts of the brain to help with pain and improve mood disorders. It blocks specific receptors in the brain, which is part of why it's effective in treating a range of conditions. Despite its benefits, there's still a lot to learn about how best to use ketamine for mental health, calling for more research to fully understand its potential.

Esketamine, a type of ketamine and marketed as "Spravato," which has been specifically approved for hard-to-treat depression, marking a significant step forward in psychiatric care. Esketamine has earned specific FDA approval for treatment-resistant depression and suicidal ideation, reflecting robust data supporting its efficacy and safety for these particular uses. The increased interest in ketamine (generic and Esketamine) for mental health treatment has spurred debates about its empirical support, especially as clinics and online health platforms begin offering it for a wide array of conditions While Esketamine is FDA approved, generic Ketamine has a solid evidence base for many disorders but does not have the FDA approval for the treatment of any mental health disorder and is therefore only prescribed off-label, emphasizing the necessity for caution in its application. Using ketamine outside of a medical setting brings up worries about safety, including the risk of becoming dependent on it. Although it's not as addictive as some drugs, the possibility of misuse and the side effects of excessive ketamine use mean that it's crucial to use it carefully, with a clear understanding of the risks and benefits.

When thinking about trying ketamine therapy, it's important to look closely at what a treatment center offers in terms of preparing for the experience, what happens during the treatment, and how they help you integrate the experience afterward. (See the section on "Finding a Quality Psychedelic Experience" later in this workbook.) Some centers might focus just on the physical effects of ketamine, while others take a more whole-person approach, considering the mental, emotional, and spiritual aspects of healing.

MDMA

MDMA, also known as ecstasy or molly, is a drug that combines the effects of stimulants and psychedelics, leading to increased energy, emotional warmth, and changes in how you sense and perceive time. It was first made in 1912 and gained attention in the 1970s when Alexander Shulgin, a chemist, saw its potential for helping with therapy. However, due to its widespread recreational use, the U.S. government banned it in the 1980s, shifting MDMA from a possible therapy tool to a controversial "party drug."

However, recent research has brought back interest in MDMA, especially for treating tough conditions like post-traumatic stress disorder and anxiety, particularly for those who haven't found relief with standard treatments. A potential game-changer for veterans and others who have lived through traumatic experiences, MDMA seems to help people talk about and process difficult memories more easily in therapy.

Fast-tracked by the FDA as a "Breakthrough Therapy," MDMA has recently completed clinical trials run by the Multidisciplinary Association for Psychedelic Studies (MAPS), which have shown promising results.

In a crushing step backward, in August 2024, the FDA declined a new drug application from Lykos Therapeutics (which used to be called MAPS PBC) that uses a specific type of MDMA, along with therapy, to help people with PTSD. This is frustrating news for veterans and others who have been looking for different ways to heal from challenging experiences. The FDA has requested an additional Phase 3 study and Lykos has begun the process of appealing the decision.

However, using MDMA comes with risks. Physically, it can cause problems like overheating, dehydration, and an imbalance in body fluids. Mentally, it can lead to anxiety or make existing mental health issues worse, particularly affecting individuals with serious mental challenges like psychosis and people in active mania with bipolar disorder. And, while it's less addictive than many drugs, there's still a risk of misuse, especially outside of controlled settings.

To reduce these risks, MDMA-assisted therapy is conducted under strict clinical guidelines. This protocol includes the presence of two therapists to ensure safety, manage the emotional and psychological landscape of the session, and optimize therapeutic outcomes. Patients undergo thorough screenings to identify any contraindications, and sessions are conducted in a controlled environment to ensure both physical safety and psychological support. For the latest research trials, multiple sessions of therapy were provided before and after each medicine session.

Psilocybin ("Magic" Mushrooms)

Psilocybin, the psychedelic compound present in over 200 mushroom species, is gaining interest for its profound psychological effects and therapeutic potential. Classified as a Schedule I drug in the United States, it is considered by the government to have a high potential for misuse with no recognized medical use, a viewpoint challenged by new research.

Referred to as "magic mushrooms," these fungi have been utilized for thousands of years across various cultures for their spiritual and healing properties, as well as the visionary states they induce. Psilocybin acts on serotonin receptors in the brain, altering mood, perception, and cognition. Ongoing studies are investigating its impact on treating mood disorders and creating a willingness to share openly, leading to therapeutic breakthroughs. This openness has been shown to produce rapid, substantial, and durable antidepressant effects, particularly notable in individuals dealing with terminal illnesses such as cancer.

Psilocybin is commonly consumed by eating dried mushrooms, mixing them into beverages, or incorporating them into edible products like chocolates. Its effects last approximately 4 to 6 hours. The psychedelic journey is often characterized as an experience of increased awareness and emotional freedom. Participants frequently report a heightened sense of connectivity with the universe and introspective clarity. These positive psychological impacts can last long after the immediate effects, contributing to sustained mental health improvements.

The U.S. Food and Drug Administration (FDA) has recognized psilocybin's promise to address Major Depressive Disorder (MDD) by designating it as a "Breakthrough Therapy." This designation accelerates the research and review process, highlighting psilocybin's significance in the field of mental health research. Research is being conducted with patients who have received a terminal diagnosis as well as otherwise healthy adults experiencing MDD. As a point of reference, there are more than 17 million people in the United States alone with MDD.

However, psilocybin use is not without risks, including potential anxiety, disorientation, and distressing hallucinations, commonly referred to as a "bad trip." While not common, sometimes these challenging experiences last for extended periods of time well beyond the day of the journey.

These risks underscore the importance of supervised consumption in therapeutic and ceremonial settings, where mental health professionals or experienced spiritual guides can help reduce the potential harms.

5-MeO-DMT (Bufo)

5-MeO-DMT, often referred to as "the God molecule" or "Bufo", is renowned for inducing an intense sense of interconnectedness and spiritual insight. This potent compound is found in certain plant species and the venom of the Bufo Alvarius toad, offering one of the most powerful psychedelic experiences known. Its rapid onset and short duration, approximately 10-20 minutes, can lead to a complete disappearance of ego and a feeling of becoming one with the universe.

5-MeO-DMT is used in modern ceremonies, retreat settings, and is gaining contemporary attention through endorsements by public figures who have shared transformative encounters facilitated by this substance. Beyond its capacity for spiritual exploration, 5-MeO-DMT shows promise in addressing psychological challenges such as depression, anxiety, and PTSD, potentially offering breakthroughs in mental health treatment by drastically improving an individual's daily outlook on life.

Despite its therapeutic potential, 5-MeO-DMT remains illegal in most places, including the United States, complicating its research and use in therapy. Ethical concerns also arise when harvesting toad venom. As a result, there has been a shift towards synthetic forms of the drug that replicate its effects without impacting the toad population.

The potent nature of 5-MeO-DMT allows one to access deep insights and foster healing. This is also why it requires respect and thoughtful engagement, a carefully considered set and setting, and the guidance of experienced guides to navigate its effects safely.

NAVIGATING CHALLENGES IN PSYCHEDELIC EXPERIENCES

For those who have faced significant challenges, psychedelic experiences can unearth deep emotions, past traumas, or profound questions about life. However, the strengths and resilience that individuals inherently possess can help navigate what arises during these journeys. Proper preparation is key to ensuring a safe, successful, and meaningful experience.

Here's how to gear up for the experience:

- **Create a Safe Space:** Psychedelic trips can be unpredictable. Setting up a calm, cozy spot ahead of time, with comforting things like tea, blankets, and soft lights, can make a big difference. Having snacks and water handy helps keep you nourished and hydrated as you go through this experience.

- **Breathe Deep:** When things get intense, breathing can be your anchor. Try deep breaths that fill your belly, hold them for a bit, then let them out slowly. Focusing on your breath can help soothe you, making it easier to face challenging moments.

- **Practice a Grounding Technique:** In moments of heightened anxiety or disconnection, grounding techniques can be really helpful. Engage in sensory grounding methods such as focusing on tactile sensations like touching a piece of soft fabric or practicing the 5-4-3-2-1 technique to reconnect with your immediate environment. These strategies help stabilize your perception and return your awareness to the present. We'll teach you more about these later in this workbook.

- **Have Someone There for You:** It's key to go through this with someone experienced or even just a trusted friend (a "sitter"). They're there to give you support, not to steer your trip. They are there to help you stay safe and get the most out of the experience.

- **It's Okay to Ask for Help:** If you need something, don't hesitate to ask your guide or sitter. They are there to help you through, but they might not always know what you need right away.

- **Open Your Eyes:** If the visuals get too much or you need to feel more grounded, just opening your eyes can help. It reconnects you to the here and now, giving you a break from the journey inside.

- **Use Positive Self-talk:** Having a go-to phrase that comforts or reassures you can be a big help in tough spots. Something that reminds you you're safe and can handle this.

- **Talk to the Psychedelic:** Yes, you can actually "talk" to the experience. Share what you're hoping for, or ask questions. It's a way to be more involved in what's happening.

- **Believe You're Safe:** Keep in your heart that you're in the right place, doing important work for yourself. This belief can be a steady base when things feel shaky.

- **Stay Curious:** Facing the challenging parts with a sense of wonder rather than fear can turn the whole experience around. Be open to learning, even from the hard stuff.

- **Plan for Afterward:** What you do after the trip, how you think about it, and how you use what you learned are super important. This is about taking those big or hard moments and finding ways to bring their lessons into your everyday life. Having a plan for this integration helps make sure the journey has a lasting positive impact.

To be extra clear, while psychedelic/entheogenic work can and often does bring profound healing, <u>it doesn't always help, and sometimes it makes matters worse.</u> While not common, people have experienced "extended difficulties" that have lasted days to years after a journey, with the extent of impairment ranging from mild to completely debilitating, sometimes with suicidality. In light of that, identifying a support network and a professional healthcare provider you can turn to in case extra support is needed is a form of insurance that is highly recommended.

Using these strategies, you can face the challenges and deep moments psychedelic experiences bring with the courage and strength you've shown in so many parts of your life. With the right mindset and support, these journeys can be a path to healing and discovering new truths about yourself.

FINDING A QUALITY PSYCHEDELIC EXPERIENCE

When choosing a psychedelic provider, the importance of thorough vetting cannot be overstated. It's essential to choose a setting and facilitators who prioritize safety, integrity, and deep healing. There are no "right" and "wrong" answers when selecting a psychedelic experience—there are many preferences and considerations unique to each individual. With the information provided here, you can find a psychedelic experience that meets your specific needs, allowing you to enter the experience with clarity and understanding of what you're getting into.

Psychedelic Experience Selection Guide
Key Questions for Your Journey:

Preparation

- **Medical and Psychological Review:** Does the provider review your health history to ensure suitability for the experience?
- **Intention Setting:** Is there guidance available to help clarify your purpose for this journey?
- **Medicine Source and Safety:** Where does the medicine come from, and is it tested for purity and safety?

During the Experience

- **Facilitator Expertise:** What experience do the facilitators have?
- **Support Ratio:** How many facilitators will be present, and what is the participant-to-facilitator ratio?
- **Setting:** What is the setting for the journey, and how does it support introspection and healing?
- **Music and Atmosphere:** Is music or any specific atmosphere provided to influence the experience?

Post-Experience Integration

- **Integration Support:** What post-journey integration support is offered?
- **Community:** Is there a community or network for ongoing support and connection?

Choosing the Right Ceremony, Retreat, or Provider

- **Reputation and Reviews:** What do reviews say about the center's reputation, and have you checked for any negative reports? Have you spoken with anyone who has worked with this provider before?
- **Facilitator Background:** Do facilitators have the necessary training and ethical standards?
- **Location and Accessibility:** How accessible is the provider based on your travel preferences and needs?
- **Amenities:** Does the center offer the amenities required for your physical and psychological comfort?

Travel Logistics

- **Travel Arrangements:** Are there specific travel arrangements or advisories to consider for the center's location?
- **Travel Logistics:** Does the center assist with or provide information on travel logistics?

Budget

- **Cost:** What is the cost range of the services, and what does it include?
- **Value for Money:** Does the provider offer amenities and experiences that justify the cost?
- **Financial Planning:** Have you considered additional costs such as travel, accommodation (if not included), and any other personal expenses?
- **Financial Aid:** If needed, is financial assistance available?

PREPARATION

"Psychedelics, used responsibly and with proper caution, would be for psychiatry what the microscope is for biology or the telescope is for astronomy. These tools make it possible to study important processes that under normal circumstances are not available for direct observation."

-Dr. Stanislav Grof, MD
Psychiatrist with 60+ years of experience
in research of non-ordinary states of consciousness

IMPORTANCE OF PREPARATION

Preparing for a psychedelic journey is about more than anticipating cool visuals; it's a deep dive into self-exploration and healing. This readiness isn't solely for the experience itself, but also for preparing you for the potential personal transformations that may follow. Embracing psychedelics signals a readiness for growth, as these experiences can unearth deep-seated emotions and offer new perspectives on life and how we view ourselves. Effective preparation of mind, body, and spirit is key to navigating and optimizing the changes these journeys can start. This process equips you with the resilience and clarity needed to integrate your insights into everyday life, making the unpredictable nature of psychedelic experiences a pathway to personal growth.

Please note:
While this workbook serves as a general guide, individuals should always prioritize and adhere to their treatment or ceremonial center's specific preparation instructions and restrictions.

MENTAL AND SPIRITUAL PREPARATION

Getting ready for a psychedelic trip means getting your mind and spirit ready for a deep dive into yourself and possible big changes. Starting to learn about psychedelics, like you're doing now, is a great first step. Knowing what might happen and what these experiences are like can make things less scary and more exciting. You might not know precisely what will happen, but learning about others' experiences can help you feel more prepared.

Here are some ways to get your mind ready:

- **Learn about the psychedelic:** Know what you're getting into. Understand how it works, what you might feel, and any risks. Being informed means you're going in with your eyes open.

- **Set clear intentions:** Think about why you're doing this. What do you hope to learn or understand better? Setting a clear goal can help guide you through the trip and make it more meaningful. We'll have some exercises on this later in the workbook.

- **See challenges as chances to grow:** Psychedelic journeys can push you out of your comfort zone. Try to see any challenging moments as opportunities to learn and grow, not just something to get through. Often, difficult moments in journeys offer the most meaningful personal breakthroughs.

- **Keep your mind calm:** When getting ready, it's important to stay as calm as possible. Try to avoid things that stress you out and do things that make you feel peaceful. Starting to meditate, even if it's just for a few minutes each day, can really help get your mind in the right place. We'll give you some meditation exercises to try later in this workbook.

Please remember, while not common, sometimes working with psychedelics/entheogens can lead to challenging experiences that linger beyond the journey day with symptoms ranging from mild impairment to completely debilitating, sometimes with suicidal thoughts. Knowing who you can turn to for support after the journey, ideally including a professional healthcare provider, is an important part of this mental preparation process.

Spiritual Alignment

Religion and spirituality, while intertwined, serve different aspects of personal growth. Religion often involves structured practices, rituals, and a community sharing the same beliefs about a higher power or God, providing a framework for worship and living according to specific doctrines. For many people, this comes with "baggage" from their childhood experiences. Spirituality, on the other hand, is more about an individual's personal relationship with the divine or the universe and does not necessarily adhere to the formal rules of any one faith. It emphasizes personal growth, inner peace, and an understanding of one's place within the wider cosmos, often focusing on the personal experience of connection and the transcendence of everyday reality.

Spiritual preparation invites you to connect with your deeper self and the universe around you. It's an opportunity to reflect on your place in the world and to establish a sacred perspective on the journey ahead. Building your own rituals or practices that honor the experience can set a tone of reverence and openness. Engaging in a form of spiritual dialogue with yourself allows for introspection on your beliefs, values, and the existential questions that guide your life. Meditation also plays a key role in spiritual readiness, quieting the mind and fostering a deep sense of connection and presence. Gratitude for the journey and the growth it promises can open your heart and mind, creating a positive and receptive mindset for the experiences to come. Again, we will provide exercises and meditations later in this workbook.

Integrating Mental and Spiritual Readiness

Combining mental preparedness with spiritual readiness ensures a comprehensive approach to your psychedelic journey. This integration facilitates a deep dive into your psyche with insight, strength, and an open heart, setting the stage for meaningful change and growth. By treating the journey as a significant opportunity for self-discovery and understanding, you prepare not just for the psychedelic experience itself but for the potential personal transformation it can catalyze.

PHYSICAL PREPARATION

Part of preparing for a psychedelic experience involves treating your body as a sacred space. Whether you've faced physical challenges in the past or are simply seeking to connect more deeply with yourself, this part of the journey focuses on aligning your body with the transformative medicine you are about to receive. It's an opportunity to become more conscious of what you consume and how you nourish your body, bringing intentionality to your everyday habits. This preparation includes making practical changes and observing how your body and mind respond, creating a foundation for a meaningful and connected experience.

Physical Preparation: Taking Care of Your Body

Health Check: Safety first. Make sure the place you're going to for your journey checks your health thoroughly. Your facilitator should know about any health issues that could make the experience risky for you. Stay away from places that don't do these checks. One best practice is to get an independent medical exam from a psychedelically-informed medical provider who is not biased by wanting to sell you a service. Dr. Ben Malcolm at www.spiritpharmacist.com and Dr. Emily Kulpa are two providers who provide psychedelic consultations. There are certainly others. It is also encouraged to get a general physical exam with your primary care provider.

Follow the "Psychedelic Diet": This special diet helps clean out your body and prepares it for the powerful nature of the psychedelic journey. **While each ceremony or program may have unique requirements**, the most common requirements for the two weeks before your trip are:

- **Eat natural, whole foods:** Skip processed stuff and go for foods that are as close to their natural state as possible. This helps clear out your system. Please stay away from protein powders as they can have ingredients in them you don't want right now.
- **Choose lighter proteins:** Heavy meats can weigh you down and are harder to process. Try eating lighter or plant-based proteins to help your body and mind feel clearer.
- **Cut out stimulants and alcohol:** Stuff like alcohol and drugs can negatively impact the experience. Cutting them out helps reset your nervous system and prepares you for an optimum psychedelic experience. Try to cut back on caffeine too.

Specific "Dieta" for Ayahuasca

The traditional use of ayahuasca is consistently paired with a specific diet. While the exact rules may differ, common principles include avoiding recreational drugs, alcohol, and sexual activity before and after the ceremony and avoiding salt, pork, spicy foods, or very cold food and beverages.

THC and Ayahuasca: There's no hard proof that THC messes with ayahuasca, but some say it can make the experience less intense. Cutting it out might help you see things more clearly.

Save Your Sexual "Energy": Traditional beliefs suggest that conserving sexual energy (including sex and masturbating before your ceremony) can enhance the spiritual and transformative potential of ayahuasca.

Take a Break from Screens: Reducing screen time before your journey can help shift your focus inward, preparing you for the introspective nature of the experience.

Avoid tyramines: Tyramines are found in fermented alcohol (red wine, beer, vermouth, sherry, etc...), fermented foods, and heavy meats. When used with ayahuasca (an MAO inhibitor), they can make the ayahuasca experience not only less effective, but actually dangerous.

Stop using cannabis: We recommend discontinuing the use of cannabis for at least two weeks (one month if you regularly work with this plant) prior to your retreat. **Cannabis use can make it difficult for many people to connect strongly with ayahuasca.**

Ayahuasca is not recommended for people with bipolar disorders as it can sometimes trigger reactions that can extend beyond the ceremony and may then require further intervention.

Ayahuasca can interact dangerously with certain medications, especially antidepressants and blood pressure medications, due to its MAOI (Monoamine oxidase inhibitor) properties. In general, it is recommended to stop most medications, if possible, four weeks in advance of an ayahuasca retreat; however, this may not be possible for all medications. Please discuss with your doctor or psychiatrist any and all medications you are taking and their interactions with MAO inhibitors, particularly if you are taking any medications that would pose a health risk to discontinue. It's not always necessary to discontinue medications, but it's very important to discuss this with your primary doctor or psychiatrist, as well as your retreat team. Discontinuing certain psychiatric medications, especially SSRIs, is a complex and lengthy process that requires careful medical supervision. This tapering process can often extend over several months.

To be extra clear, some medications are **contraindicated** with ayahuasca medicine. Unlike food interactions, whose consequences are usually unlikely to be serious, interaction with pharmaceutical drugs and medications (including some over-the-counter medicines and certain herbs) **can be potentially life-threatening**. In particular, the following drugs and medications can be dangerous with ayahuasca and should be discontinued at least four weeks prior to partaking in an ayahuasca ceremony:

- Other MAOIs
- SSRIs (any selective serotonin reuptake inhibitor)
- Antihypertensives (high blood pressure medicine)
- Appetite suppressants (diet pills)
- Medicine for bronchitis; antihistamines, medicines for colds, sinus problems, hay fever, or allergies (Actifed DM, Benadryl, Benylin, Chlor-Trimeton, Compoz, Bromarest-DM or -DX, Dimetane-DX cough syrup, Dristan Cold & Flu, Phenergan with dextromethorphan, Robitussin-DM, Vicks Formula 44-D, several Tylenol cold, cough, and flu preparations, and many others).
- Any drug containing dextromethorphan/ DXM or with DM, DX, or Tuss in its name.
- CNS (central nervous system) depressants (Xanax, Ativan, etc)
- Vasodilators
- Antipsychotics

- Mood stabilizers such as Lithium
- Barbiturates
- Cocaine
- Amphetamines (meth-, dex-, amphetamine), ephedrine, MDMA (Ecstasy), MDA, MDEA, PMA
- Opiates (heroin, morphine, codeine, and especially opium)
- Dextromethorphan (DXM)
- Mescaline (any phenethylamine) – less dangerous but not recommended
- Kratom – less dangerous but not recommended
- Kava – less dangerous but not recommended
- Herbal supplements St. John´s Wort & 5-HTP

What Else Can You Learn from the Dieta?

Starting any "Dieta" might be the first time you really think deeply about your habits and inner life. This change in how you see things is a big part of getting ready. You might feel like everything's lining up or falling apart. That's okay; it means you're on the right path.

When you struggle to give something up, like coffee, it's a chance to see what's really going on. Maybe you've been using it to hide from your feelings. Seeing this can be a big moment.

This deep look at yourself is important, including understanding your habits and what they're covering up, and is part of getting ready for a psychedelic journey. It's not just about seeing your habits but understanding why they're there. That's where you'll find the real reasons you're looking for healing.

The "Dieta" is also a test of your willpower. If you slip up or find it hard, that's normal. It's a chance to think about how strong your will is, like working out a muscle.

HOMELIFE AND RELATIONSHIP PREPARATION

Preparing your home and relationships is another step for establishing a supportive recovery environment after your psychedelic experience. This isn't just about making your physical space look nice; it's about creating a safe and understanding "space" for emotional and spiritual healing. Here are some ideas to make sure your environment and relationships help you heal:

- **Create a Calm Space for Reflection:** Choose a quiet and comfortable area in your home where you can think and recover after your experience. This spot should be peaceful, with things that help you feel relaxed and introspective. Having a secure place to process your thoughts without interruption is ideal.

- **Make Your Living Space Peaceful:** Clean and organize your home to reflect a clear and calm mind. A tidy space can help you transition more smoothly from your psychedelic journey back to everyday life. Add things that make your home feel alive and inspiring, like plants or personal items that bring you joy.

- **Remove Triggers for Addictions:** If part of your journey involves overcoming an addiction, it's important to remove any substances, tools related to their use, and anything else that might remind you of it from your home. Creating an environment free of these triggers can help you focus on your recovery without unnecessary temptations.

- **Talk Openly with Family and Friends:** Let those close to you know about your plans and what you hope to achieve. This conversation helps build a support system that understands and respects your healing process. It's essential for those around you to know how they can help.

- **Be Honest About Your Needs:** Tell your trusted friends or family about the changes you're trying to make and the difficulties you might face. Open discussions about your feelings invite support and provide a sense of accountability and understanding.

- **Find a Support Group:** Connect with people who have gone through similar experiences, who understand your journey. As you heal, this group can offer valuable insights and a sense of belonging.

- **Set Clear Boundaries:** Make sure you have the privacy or company you need when you need it by setting boundaries with yourself and others. This helps you manage your time and energy during recovery.

- **Show Gratitude:** Regularly thank your support network for their help and love. Recognizing their contribution to your healing strengthens your relationships and builds a foundation of mutual respect.

By carefully preparing your living space and strengthening your relationships, you're building an environment that supports your journey to healing. Acknowledging the need for a supportive setting is a critical step toward embracing the changes that come with psychedelic exploration and recovery.

SUPPLEMENT USE

Many people are curious about the role of supplements in preparing for and recovering from a psychedelic experience. While there's no direct research correlating the use of supplements with the enhancement or safety of one's experience, anecdotal advice from professionals in the space offers some recommendations. It's essential to remember that any changes in diet or the introduction of supplements should be approached with care and, if possible, under the guidance of a healthcare professional.

Guided by Nature Approach:

- **Nature's Embrace:** Before and after the psychedelic experience, immerse yourself in nature. This grounding experience can be vital for mental well-being. The sun's natural light is believed to aid in the production of serotonin, potentially enhancing mood and promoting a sense of calm.

- **Restorative Rest:** If you feel fatigued after the psychedelic experience, allow your body the rest it craves. Sleep is immensely healing, and a short nap can be rejuvenating.

- **Fundamental Pillars:** Whether or not you choose to incorporate supplements, always return to the basics for holistic well-being: adequate rest, moments of reflection, good nutrition, and plenty of water.

Anecdotal Recommendations:

The following supplement suggestions are commonly recommended and intended to support overall well-being and recovery:

Use 1 Week Before and for 2-3 Days After:

- **NAC:** Believed to offer antioxidant support and to be beneficial for liver health.

- **Vitamin C (1000 mg):** An essential vitamin with antioxidant properties.

- **Vitamin E (450 mg or 1000 IU):** May help reduce oxidative stress in the body.

- **Alpha Lipoic Acid (600 mg):** Often considered an antioxidant compound.
- **Magnesium (preferably Magnesium L-Threonate):** Essential for various biochemical reactions in the body and may promote relaxation.

After the Psychedelic Experience (use for 2-3 Days):

- **5HTP:** Wait at least 24 hours after the experience before introducing 5HTP, as it's a precursor to serotonin and can influence mood.
- **Melatonin (5-10mg before bed):** Naturally produced in the body, melatonin can help regulate sleep-wake cycles. It might be beneficial if you find it challenging to sleep post-psychedelic experience.

Supplements to Avoid:

It's crucial not to take certain supplements around the time of your psychedelic experience due to potential interactions or adverse effects:

- Avoid 5HTP on the day of the psychedelic experience.
- Do not consume St. John's wort.

The effectiveness and safety of these supplements can vary depending on the type of psychedelic used. It's important to understand that what works well in conjunction with one substance may not be appropriate with another. Always discuss the specific supplement you plan to use with your healthcare provider and/or facilitator.

Remember, while the above recommendations are based on anecdotal evidence and are not comprehensive, it's always crucial to listen to your body and your medical provider. Everyone's journey is unique, and what might benefit one person might not necessarily resonate with another.

REFLECTIVE JOURNALING EXERCISES

Journaling is a powerful tool for anyone seeking to reflect on their life journey and personal experiences. It offers a way to look inward and better understand your thoughts, feelings, and the events that have shaped you. These exercises are designed to help you explore where you've been, how those experiences have influenced you, and where you want to go from here. Rather than treating these prompts as just another task to complete, approach them with intention and curiosity, as if embarking on a journey to discover more about yourself.

The goal of this process is to find a few key goals or intentions that will guide you as you explore the possibilities of psychedelic experiences.

Remember, there's no "right" way to do this. Feel free to express your thoughts through writing, drawing, or any form that feels right. If a question feels too hard, it's okay to skip it and come back later or explore it in small parts.

General Life Reflections:

Life Satisfaction Matrix: Please find the Life Satisfaction Tracker on page 162 and take a few minutes to complete the pre-psychedelic rating and reflect on your strengths and areas of opportunity as you prepare for your psychedelic experience. You will complete this again each week following your psychedelic experience.

What events have led you to this moment in your life? Try to think about the big moments or changes that brought you here. If reflecting on this feels overwhelming, take it one step at a time.

What do you hope to understand or discover? Think about what you hope to discover or understand better about yourself or your life. This can include both challenges and areas where you've felt successful.

Where do you feel stressed or uneasy in your life? Identify areas in your life where you feel tension.

_____

_____

_____

_____

_____

_____

_____

_____

_____

_____

_____

_____

_____

_____

_____

_____

_____

_____

_____

_____

_____

_____

_____

_____

Are there things in your life that need your attention but have yet to be addressed? Consider unresolved issues or concerns.

What hurts or challenges from your younger years are still affecting you?
Reflect on any difficult experiences from childhood or adolescence.

Personal Aspirations and Challenges:

What positive changes or goals do you want to bring into your life? Think about what you want to achieve or improve. Remember, small steps are key; every little bit of progress counts.

What big challenge are you dealing with right now that you wish you could see differently? Describe a current problem where a new perspective could help.

If you could let go of one thing, what would it be? Think about something you're ready to release or move on from.

Are there any habits or behaviors you want to change? Identify any patterns you wish were different in your life.

Self-Perception and Regrets:

How do you view yourself? Share your feelings about yourself, including both strengths and areas you're working to improve. Balancing your view by recognizing your resilience and accomplishments is just as important as acknowledging areas of growth.

Do you have regrets or things you wish had gone differently? What makes you feel ashamed? Reflect on past regrets or moments of shame.

Interpersonal Dynamics:

What fears do you have? What makes you defensive? Are you holding onto any hard feelings? As you reflect on these questions, remember it's okay to approach this slowly. Acknowledge your feelings, and consider also reflecting on how you've navigated past fears or conflicts.

Have you hurt others? How? Think about times you may have caused pain to someone else.

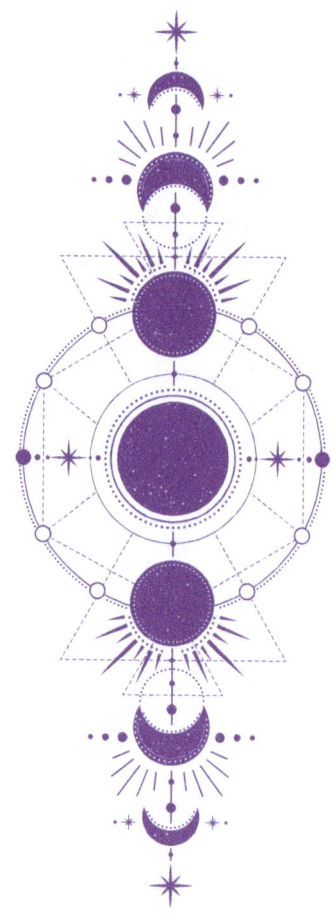

DISCOVERING YOUR INTENTION EXERCISES

As you move forward from jotting down your thoughts and feelings, you've likely started to see things about yourself a bit more clearly. Now's the moment to shape that understanding into clear goals or wishes for what's ahead. Think of setting an intention like picking a destination for a trip. It gives you a reason for going and something to aim for. These next steps are here to help you take what you've discovered about yourself in the reflective journaling and turn it into specific hopes for what you want to get out of this experience. These intentions should resonate with your unique experiences and your specific challenges.

Each of the example intentions below is designed to resonate deeply with specific experiences. They focus on healing, acceptance, and growth, aiming to provide a meaningful direction for the psychedelic journey ahead.

Once you have formulated your intention in sentence form, try distilling it into a four or five-word mantra. This mantra should capture the essence of your intention and be easy to recall and repeat. It can serve as a grounding tool during your journey and as a focal point in your daily life.

Overcoming Trauma

- **Original Intention:** Show me how to find peace with my past actions and the actions I witnessed, and lead me towards understanding and acceptance.
  Simplified Mantra: "Find peace and understanding."

- **Original Intention:** Illuminate a path through my trauma, showing me the strength in my vulnerability and guiding me toward healing.
  Simplified Mantra: "Illuminate healing paths."

- **Original Intention:** Help me to break free from the grip of my past traumas to live more fully in the present without fear.
  Simplified Mantra: "Live fully, fearlessly."

- **Original Intention:** Reveal to me how I can transform my traumatic experiences into sources of resilience and empathy.
  Simplified Mantra: "Transform trauma into strength."

Adapting to Mental and/or Physical Limitations

- **Original Intention:** Assist me in finding new ways to adapt to and compensate for my challenges due to my brain injury, enhancing my quality of life.
  Simplified Mantra: "Adapt and enhance life."

- **Original Intention:** Guide me in understanding the changes in my cognitive and emotional landscape and show me how to embrace these changes positively.
  Simplified Mantra: "Embrace change positively."

- **Original Intention:** Help me strengthen the neural pathways that remain, enhancing my brain's plasticity and aiding in my recovery process.
  Simplified Mantra: "Strengthen and recover."

- **Original Intention:** Show me how to accept my body's limitations while recognizing its strengths, fostering a new relationship with my physical self.
  Simplified Mantra: "Accept and value self.

- **Original Intention:** Help me find the courage to adapt to my physical changes and discover new ways to experience joy and fulfillment.
  Simplified Mantra: "Find joy in adaptation."

- **Original Intention:** Illuminate the path to healing by guiding me in understanding the connection between my physical pain and emotional well-being and how one can influence the other.
  Simplified Mantra: "Connect pain and peace."

Finding My Purpose

- **Original Intention:** Guide me in reconciling my previous career with my new life, helping me to integrate these experiences into a cohesive self-identity.
  Simplified Mantra: "Integrate service and self."

- **Original Intention:** Help me understand myself and my purpose more deeply.
  Simplified Mantra: "Understand self deeply.

Forgiving Myself

- **Original Intention:** Guide me on the path to truly forgiving and letting go of old hurts so I can have a heart full of love, understanding, and peace.
  Simplified Mantra: "Forgive and love."

Living Mindfully

- **Original Intention:** Teach me how to let go of old stories and beliefs that aren't helping me grow.
  Simplified Mantra: "Let go and grow."

- **Original Intention:** Show me how to live in the now, to be mindful and at peace.
  Simplified Mantra: "Live in the now."

- **Original Intention:** Show me what I need to change in myself to be more genuine and to share my true self with the world.
  Simplified Mantra: "Be genuine. Share me."

Strengthening Relationships

- **Original Intention:** Help me rediscover the sense of camaraderie I used to feel in my current relationships and community.
  Simplified Mantra: "Rediscover camaraderie everywhere."

- **Original Intention:** Help me learn to love myself and others without holding back.
  Simplified Mantra: "Love freely. Love me.."

- **Original Intention:** Help me see what needs to heal in my friendships and relationships, and teach me how to build stronger, loving connections.
  Simplified Mantra: "Heal and connect."

Facing My Fears

- **Original Intention:** Point out the parts of my life that I need to change to be more in tune with who I really am.
  Simplified Mantra: "Align life with self."

- **Original Intention:** Help me find the wisdom inside me so I can trust my gut feelings more.
  Simplified Mantra: "Trust inner wisdom."

- **Original Intention:** Shine a light on what scares me and help me find ways to get past those fears.
  Simplified Mantra: "Illuminate and overcome."

My Intentions

Document your top 1-3 intentions here. Keep them concise and impactful.

Top Intention 1:

_____

_____

_____

_____

_____

_____

Top Intention 2:

_____

_____

_____

_____

_____

Top Intention 3:

_____

_____

_____

_____

_____

_____

IDENTIFYING YOUR SUPPORT EXERCISES

For those stepping into a journey of integration and healing, pinpointing and rallying your circle of support is essential. This section aims to help you recognize the multiple layers of support you have, pulling from your inner strengths, people and places around you, and even broader spiritual or universal forces. By mapping out these supports, you're not just preparing for a psychedelic journey; you're building a comprehensive support system for every aspect of your life's journey.

External Support is all about the concrete, real-world help you can lean on. This might include friends who've been through similar experiences, family members who've got your back, healthcare professionals who understand your specific issues, groups that offer a sense of belonging, and peaceful natural spots that provide a quiet space for reflection. Don't forget pets; they're amazing companions, giving unconditional love and a sense of calm.

My External Support:

Inner Support focuses on the personal strengths and abilities you've developed throughout your life, which equip you to navigate life's ups and downs. This includes the resilience built by overcoming challenges, problem-solving skills sharpened in difficult situations, adaptability in facing new scenarios, a sense of humor to lighten tough moments, and the self-kindness that is essential for your healing and growth.

My Inner Support:

Transpersonal Support looks beyond the individual to the broader, often spiritual, connections that offer a sense of meaning and connection to the bigger picture. Many people draw strength from activities that link them to a larger purpose or the natural world, whether through meditation, spiritual or religious practices, the awe-inspiring beauty of nature, or rituals that bring a sense of stability and focus. Sources such as motivational books, energy healing, or physical-spiritual practices like yoga or martial arts can also provide deep and sustaining support for this journey.

My Transpersonal Support:

MEDITATION EXERCISES

Developing a habit of meditation is like finding a peaceful spot in the middle of a busy day. It's a way to take a deep breath, watch your thoughts as they come and go, and just be calm for a while. This creates a quiet space inside your mind that can help heal both your thoughts and feelings. **This does not need to be a long process- it is more effective to do 5-10 minutes each day rather than an hour-long session once per week.**

This skill of sustained, non-judgmental attention (meditation) in psychedelic work is important for multiple reasons. First, it enhances your ability to attentively observe your inner thoughts and feelings while using the psychedelic without becoming overwhelmed by them. Second, it trains you to maintain a mindful state after the psychedelic experience, helping integrate the insights and emotional shifts experienced during psychedelic sessions.

For those seeking a straightforward and accessible text-based tool for mindfulness and mental well-being, Take2Minutes.org is a highly recommended resource that I helped create. They offer a variety of activities, including daily positive messages, daily and instant meditations, anxiety-specific meditations, breathing exercises, a gratitude journal, and sleep audio. What makes **Take2Minutes.org** an exceptionally cool tool compared with others is it is text-based. 92% of text messages are read within three minutes, ensuring that these mindfulness exercises truly reach and engage you in real time. Readers of this book can start with a **15-day full-access free trial**, experiencing the benefits firsthand. After the trial, continued access is available at a **50% discount using the code "MIND." To get started, you can simply text JOIN to (717) 674-2779 in the U.S. or (778) 400-0444 in Canada.**

In addition, there are numerous other apps that you can consider. Insight Timer, Calm, Headspace, and Waking Up are just a few.

To start, pick any of the following meditations and see how it feels for you.

Breath Awareness Meditation:

This meditation focuses on noticing your breath, a simple yet powerful way to cultivate calm and focus. It offers a moment of quiet amidst the busyness of life, helping you feel more grounded and present in the here and now.

- **Starting Out:** Close your eyes and let yourself settle into a quiet space. Focus on your breath, the steady rhythm that's always with you.

- **Watch Your Breath**: Pay attention to how your breath flows in and out, how your chest rises and falls, and how the air feels cool as you breathe in and warm as you breathe out. Let your breath be your anchor, keeping you centered.

- **Let Go of Tension**: Imagine that with every breath out, you're letting go of any stress or tough memories. Each exhale is a chance to feel a bit lighter.

- **Come Back to the Breath:** If your mind wanders off, gently bring your thoughts back to your breathing. This is a way to stay in the here and now, showing your inner strength.

- **Find Peace:** Keep breathing with attention, feeling how each breath in gives you life and each breath out releases what you don't need. This moment of breathing deeply is your peace, away from life's noise.

- **Ending the Meditation:** Slowly open your eyes, keeping the calm and focus you've found. Let this feeling of being centered stay with you as you go about your day. Your breath is a tool for peace and strength, ready for you whenever you need it.

Box Breathing Meditation:

Box breathing is a simple relaxation technique that helps you focus and relieve stress. It's especially useful when you need to calm your mind and body. Here's how to do it:

- **Find a Seat:** Sit in a comfortable position with your back straight and feet flat on the ground.

- **Close Your Eyes:** Gently close your eyes to eliminate distractions.

- **Inhale:** Slowly breathe in through your nose while counting to four. Imagine filling your lungs with air completely.

- **Hold:** Keep your breath for four seconds. Enjoy a moment of stillness.

- **Exhale:** Slowly breathe out through your mouth for four seconds, releasing all the air and any tension.

- **Hold Again:** Pause for four seconds after exhaling to complete one cycle of box breathing.

- **Repeat:** Continue this pattern—inhale, hold, exhale, hold—for several cycles. Focus solely on your breathing.

- **Conclude:** After a few minutes, or when you feel more relaxed, gently open your eyes.

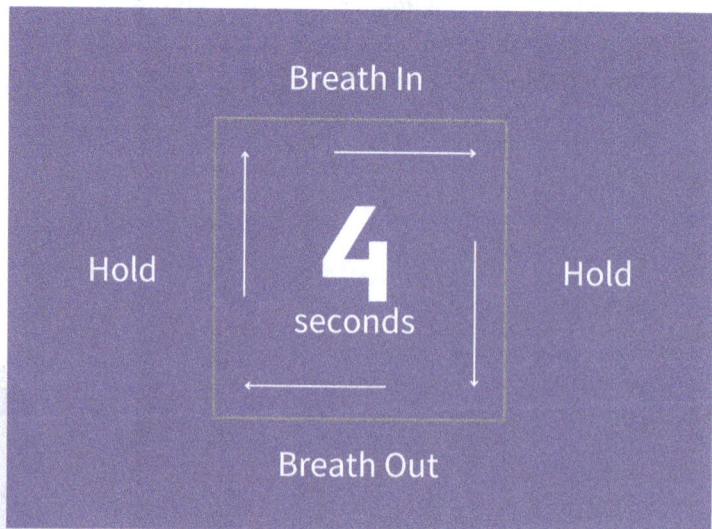

Candle Gaze Meditation:

This meditation uses a candle flame to help find peace and focus. It's a way to quiet your mind and remind yourself of your inner strength and calm. **This meditation is particularly effective when done for 5 minutes before going to sleep or when trying to calm yourself.**

- **Getting Started:** Light a candle and put it where you can easily see it without straining. Let this flame catch all your attention, symbolizing the steady light inside you, always shining through life's ups and downs.

- **Watch the Flame:** Look at the candle's flame, seeing how it moves and changes. Notice the different colors at its heart and how it reacts to the air—just like we respond to life around us. This dance of the flame can teach us to be flexible and strong.

- **Stay in the Moment:** By focusing on the flame, let yourself be fully here and now. The flame's constant change is a reminder to stay present, even when thoughts of the past or future come up. Watching it closely helps you learn to stay steady amidst change.

- **Finding Focus Again:** If you get distracted or your thoughts wander, bring your attention back to the flame. This is like finding your balance again, a skill you've practiced in challenging times and now in quiet moments.

- **Feel Connected:** Imagine that the warmth and light from the flame are part of you. Feeling connected to the flame helps remind us that we're all part of something bigger, sharing the same spark of life.

- **Carrying Peace With You:** When you finish, remember the sense of calm and focus you found. Even after the candle is out, imagine its light stays with you, a symbol of hope and inner peace as you move through your day.

Body Scan Meditation:

This meditation is about getting back in touch with yourself. It's a way to thank your body for all it's gone through and recognize both the pain and the strength it holds.

- **Starting Point:** Begin with your feet and slowly work your way up. As you focus on each part of your body, think about how much it's done for you. Appreciate your body's incredible ability to heal and keep going, even when things are tough.

- **Moving Through Your Body:** Starting with the top of your head, move your attention slowly down, exploring each part of your body with gentle interest. Notice how each area feels, the signs of strength you find, and any discomfort or tension. Imagine your focus as something soothing, offering comfort as you go.

- **Offering Healing:** If you come across any spots that hurt or feel tight, approach them with kindness. Picture your breath as healing energy going right to these spots, easing pain and relaxing tightness, filling every part of you with new life.

- **Feeling Whole:** After you've paid attention to your whole body, take a moment to feel the unity within. Think about everything your body has been through—all the marks and pains are signs of your resilience. This complete acceptance is a way to celebrate your body's ability to heal itself.

- **Closing with Gratitude:** End your body scan by quietly thanking your body for always being there for you. This meditation is a step towards making peace with your body, promising to listen to it more and care for it with more understanding and kindness.

Loving Kindness Meditation:

This meditation is about learning to open your heart more, to be kind in a way that starts with those close to you and slowly includes everyone, even yourself. It's a way to remember how strong love is, no matter what life throws at you.

- **Think of Someone Special:** Imagine someone you love easily, like a family member, close friend, or even a pet. Choose someone whose thought makes you smile without effort.

- **Wish Them Well:** Hold their image in your mind. Look at their face, their smile, the spark in their eyes. While thinking of them, silently wish for their happiness. You could say in your mind, "I hope you're happy," or "I want joy and happiness for you."

- **Picture Their Happiness:** Believe that your good wishes reach them. See a smile light up their face, showing true happiness. Feel how this makes your heart warm, spreading kindness and love.

- **Spread the Kindness:** Let this warm feeling grow from your heart. Picture it wrapping around both of you, showing the strong, loving connection you share.

- **Be Kind to Yourself:** Now, send some of that kindness to yourself. With each breath in and out, wish for your own happiness and peace. Say, "I hope I'm happy," or "May I have peace." Let yourself take in these good wishes, filling up with the same kindness you have for others.

Grounding Exercises

Grounding techniques are practical strategies designed to help individuals reconnect with the present moment, particularly useful when feeling overwhelmed, anxious, or detached. These methods bring awareness back to the here and now by engaging the senses, body, and mind.

Sensory Grounding Techniques

Focus on sensory experiences to ground yourself:

- **Taste:** Suck on a sour candy, chew gum, or taste something with a strong flavor.
- **Touch:** Handle a stress ball, brush your hair, or pet an animal.
- **Sound:** Listen to various types of music like calming classical tunes or natural sounds.
- **Sight:** Observe calming images or watch a serene video.
- **5-4-3-2-1 Technique:** Notice and name 5 things you can see, 4 you can touch, 3 you can hear, 2 you can smell, and 1 you can taste.

Physical Grounding Techniques

Engage your body to return to the present:

- **Deep Breathing:** Focus on slow, deep breaths.
- **Progressive Muscle Relaxation:** Tense and relax each muscle group.
- **Simple Physical Actions:** Splash cold water on your face or hold a piece of ice.

Cognitive Grounding Techniques

Manage your thoughts to stay grounded:

- **Positive Reminiscence:** Think about a happy memory.
- **Counting Games:** Count backwards from 100 by sevens.
- **Recitation:** Recite a poem or a song lyric that you enjoy.

Personalizing Your Approach

Experiment with different techniques to discover what works best for you. Modify these strategies according to your environment and preferences, ensuring they are always accessible when needed.

Progressive Muscle Relaxation

Progressive Muscle Relaxation (PMR) is a deep relaxation technique that helps decrease stress and physical tension by systematically tensing and relaxing different muscle groups. This practice not only aids in stress relief but also enhances mindfulness and body awareness.

Steps for Progressive Muscle Relaxation

1. Preparation:

- Find a quiet, comfortable place where you won't be disturbed.
- Sit or lie down in a comfortable position.
- Close your eyes and take a few deep breaths, inhaling through your nose and exhaling through your mouth.

2. Tensing and Relaxing Muscle Groups:

- Work through your body, one muscle group at a time. Tense each muscle group for about 5-10 seconds, then relax for 15-20 seconds before moving to the next group.
- Focus on the difference between the feeling of tension and relaxation:
  - **Feet:** Curl toes downward to tense; relax to release.
  - **Lower Legs:** Pull toes toward shins to tense; relax to soften.
  - **Thighs:** Squeeze thigh muscles; relax to let go.
  - **Buttocks:** Tighten buttocks; relax to ease tension.
  - **Stomach:** Draw in the stomach tightly; relax to expand.
  - **Chest**: Deeply inhale to expand the chest; exhale to relax.
  - **Back:** Gently arch the back; relax to return to neutral.
  - **Hands:** Clench fists; open hands to relax.
  - **Arms:** Tense biceps by bending elbows; relax and straighten.
  - **Shoulders:** Shrug towards the ears; relax to lower.
  - **Neck:** Gently press head back or forward; relax to neutral.
  - **Face:** Scrunch the features tightly; relax to smooth out.

3. Final Relaxation:

- Take a few more deep breaths, focusing on the feeling of relaxation spreading through your body.
- Stay in this relaxed state for a few moments, enjoying the sensation.

Throughout the process, adjust the tension and relaxation phases according to your comfort level. Please avoid straining, especially if you have any existing injuries or health conditions.

Finish your session with some light stretching or a brief walk to gently transition back to daily activities while maintaining this new state of relaxation.

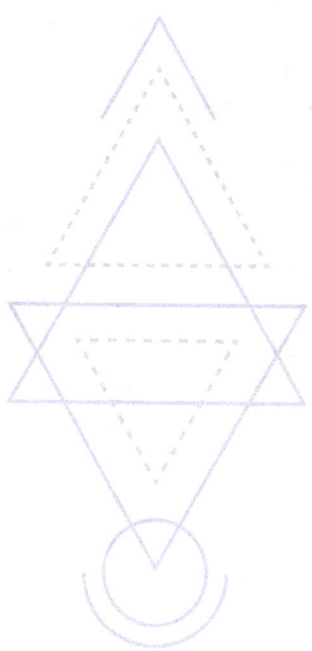

PACKING ESSENTIALS FOR A PSYCHEDELIC RETREAT

Here's a guide tailored to ensure you can immerse yourself fully in the healing experience, with peace of mind regarding your worldly concerns. (We'll give you a checklist you can use later.)

Documentation and Finances:

- **Travel Documents:** Secure digital copies of your passport and travel documents. Email them to yourself and keep physical copies in each piece of luggage.

- **Luggage Identification:** Clearly label all luggage with your contact information for both your destination and home.

- **Financial Readiness:** Ensure you have adequate funds in the local currency. Check the condition of bills if bringing cash and confirm your PIN is compatible with international ATMs. Notify your bank and cell provider of your travel plans.

Personal Affairs:

- **Home Responsibilities:** Assign a trusted individual to manage your home affairs, like pet care, plant watering, or childcare. Ensuring these are handled allows you to focus on your retreat experience.

- **Financial Responsibilities:** Arrange to have all bills paid in advance or set up automatic payments to ensure all financial commitments are met while you are away. This preparation prevents any disruptions or concerns about overdue payments, allowing you to fully engage in your retreat without worry.

Communication and Safety:

- **Emergency Contacts:** Keep emergency information on you at all times.

- **Cell Phone Use:** You can bring your phone, but most retreats require that you keep it off for the duration of the retreat.

- **Travel Companion:** When traveling out of the country, ideally travel with a trusted friend. Traveling alone can be psychologically stressful and, sometimes, dangerous.

Language and Cultural Respect:

- **Basic Phrases:** Learn key phrases in the local language to show respect and enhance your experience.
- **Cultural Sensitivity:** Research and respect local customs, understanding that you are a guest in another country.

Health and Comfort:

- **Hydration:** Carry a quality water bottle and consider portable purification methods if needed. Please do not drink or brush your teeth with tap water.
- **Sun and Insect Protection:** Pack non-toxic sunblock, sunglasses, a hat, and natural insect repellent. Consider long sleeves and mosquito-proof clothing for additional protection.
- **Medical Precautions:** Bring necessary prescription and non-prescription medications, and consult with a healthcare provider about recommended vaccines or anti-malaria measures. Ensure medications do not conflict with your retreat substances. Please bring a copy of your prescriptions as an extra precaution.

Apparel and Gear:

- **Adaptable Clothing:** Choose quick-drying, breathable attire suitable for fluctuating temperatures. Pack a variety of layers, including warm clothes for cooler nights. Don't forget your bathing suit!
- **Footwear:** Opt for comfortable, easy-to-slip-on shoes or sandals, as many retreat centers have a no-shoes policy indoors. Sturdy sandals or waterproof boots are also recommended if you plan on venturing into natural surroundings or if the retreat involves walking in nature.
- **Headgear:** A bandana or hair ties can manage hair during windy rides or during intense retreat sessions.
- **Lighting:** Bring a headlamp or flashlight with a red light setting for nighttime navigation without disturbing others.

Toiletries and Accessories:

- **Eco-friendly Toiletries:** Select biodegradable products to minimize environmental impact. A versatile soap can serve multiple cleaning purposes.

Items for the Altar

- **Personal Memento:** A personal item that holds significant meaning, such as a photograph, a small keepsake, or a symbol of your intention for the retreat. This item will serve as a touchstone for your journey and can anchor you during moments of deep introspection. Mementos could be a military insignia, a family heirloom, or even a piece of natural element like a stone or shell from a place with special memories.

Personal Items:

- **Journaling:** Pack this journal and pens/pencils for recording and reflecting on your experiences.
- **Leisure:** Include a book or two for quiet daytime moments, avoiding an overload of electronic devices to embrace digital detox.

If Bringing a Service Dog:

- **Supportive Gear:** If you have a service dog, bring their essentials and any necessary documentation. (Service dogs can be great companions in psychedelic journeys.)

Protective Measures:

- **Waterproofing:** Keep waterproof bags handy to shield your belongings from sudden downpours.

What to Leave Behind:

- **Valuables:** Avoid bringing items that are expensive or hold sentimental value.
- **Excess Tech:** Limit technology to essentials, like a camera or phone, to connect with nature and self.
- **Alcohol, Cannabis, and any non-prescribed medication.**
- **Weapons of any kind** (including personal knife and/or multi-tool).
- **Makeup:** Embrace the retreat as an opportunity to be au naturel.

By packing mindfully, you can create a foundation of ease for your journey. The key is to balance practical needs with the intent to disconnect and dive into the transformative experience. Whether you're venturing into the heart of the jungle or finding solace in a retreat center, these essentials will help you maintain focus on your inner work and healing. Remember, this is more than a trip; it's a step toward personal discovery and growth.

CHECKLISTS

Comprehensive Health Screening:

- [ ] Ensure a thorough health evaluation is conducted
- [ ] Be transparent about your medical history for a safe journey.

Embrace the 'Dieta' for three weeks before your psychedelic experience:

- [ ] Commit to whole, organic food choices.
- [ ] Avoid processed foods, additives, and protein powders.
- [ ] Choose lighter proteins and avoid pork and red meat.
- [ ] Abstain from alcohol and recreational drugs, and reduce caffeine intake.
- [ ] Maintain hydration with water and natural juices.
- [ ] Practice mindful eating and listening to your body's needs.
- [ ] Incorporate a variety of fruits, vegetables, and grains.
- [ ] Moderate the use of salt and spices, flavoring herbs.
- [ ] No pickled, fermented, or smoked foods.
- [ ] No overly ripped foods.
- [ ] No dairy.
- [ ] Caffeine (weaned off one week out)
- [ ] Limit nicotine (vaping, patches, cigarettes, or pouch/dipping.)

Specific Considerations for People with Prescriptions:

- [ ] Consult with a healthcare professional to safely discontinue any conflicting medications, especially antidepressants (SSRIs), MAO inhibitors, sleep aids, barbiturates, and blood pressure medications.

Lifestyle Adjustments:

- [ ] Consider abstaining from cannabis (THC) to avoid potential diminishment of the experience.
- [ ] Conserve sexual energy by abstaining from sex and masturbation. Initiate a digital detox, reducing exposure to news and social media.

Medication Adjustments:

In particular, the following drugs and medications can be dangerous with ayahuasca and should be discontinued at least four weeks prior to partaking in an ayahuasca ceremony:

- [ ] Other MAOIs
- [ ] SSRIs (any selective serotonin reuptake inhibitor)
- [ ] Antihypertensives (high blood pressure medicine)
- [ ] Appetite suppressants (diet pills)
- [ ] Medicine for bronchitis; antihistamines, medicines for colds, sinus problems, hay fever, or allergies (Actifed DM, Benadryl, Benylin, Chlor-Trimeton, Compoz, Bromarest-DM or -DX, Dimetane-DX cough syrup, Dristan Cold & Flu, Phenergan with dextromethorphan, Robitussin-DM, Vicks Formula 44-D, several Tylenol cold, cough, flu preparations, and many others.
- [ ] Any drug containing dextromethorphan/ DXM or with DM, DX, or Tuss in its name.
- [ ] CNS (central nervous system) depressants (Xanax, Ativan, etc)
- [ ] Vasodilators
- [ ] Antipsychotics
- [ ] Mood stabilizers like Lithium
- [ ] Barbiturates
- [ ] Cocaine
- [ ] Amphetamines (meth-, dex-, amphetamine), ephedrine, MDMA (Ecstasy), MDA, MDEA, PMA
- [ ] Opiates (heroin, morphine, codeine, and especially opium)
- [ ] Dextromethorphan (DXM)
- [ ] Mescaline (any phenethylamine) – less dangerous but not recommended
- [ ] Kratom – less dangerous but not recommended
- [ ] Kava – less dangerous but not recommended
- [ ] Herbal supplements St. John's Wort & 5-HTP

Homelife and Relationship Preparation Checklist

☐ **Designate a Peaceful Integration Space:** Choose a tranquil area in your home dedicated to reflection and integration, ensuring it's equipped for comfort and healing.

☐ **Harmonize Your Living Environment:** Declutter and cleanse your living spaces to promote clarity and renewal. Add elements like plants or artwork that contribute to a positive, vibrant environment.

☐ **Communicate Openly with Loved Ones:** Discuss your intentions and what you hope to achieve with the psychedelic journey, fostering understanding and support.

☐ **Clarify Your Intentions and Seek Support:** Have honest conversations with trusted individuals about your goals and the support you need, inviting them to be a part of your healing process.

☐ **Build a Supportive Community:** Engage with groups or individuals who share similar experiences and can offer support and companionship.

☐ **Establish Boundaries for Healing:** Define clear personal and relational boundaries to protect your integration process and ensure you have the necessary space and time.

☐ **Practice Gratitude and Appreciation:** Regularly express thanks to those who support you, recognizing their contribution to your journey towards healing.

Packing Checklist

Documentation and Finances:

- [ ] Digital and physical copies of passport, travel documents, and travel itinerary.
- [ ] Luggage tags with contact information.
- [ ] Notified bank and cell provider of travel plans.
- [ ] $100-$200 USD to purchase local crafts on the last day of the retreat (optional but highly recommended).
- [ ] $50 Local currency or plan to go to an ATM after landing to be used to tip staff (optional but highly recommended).
- [ ] Secure travel medical insurance (optional but highly recommended).

Personal Affairs:

- [ ] Arrangements for home responsibilities (pets, plants, childcare).
- [ ] Arrange to have all bills paid in advance or set up automatic payments.

Communication and Safety:

- [ ] List of emergency contacts.
- [ ] Plan for cell phone use (international plans/local SIM cards).
- [ ] Provide emergency contact information and procedures to a family member or loved one so they can reach you if necessary.

Language and Cultural Respect:

- [ ] Basic phrases in the local language.
- [ ] Research on local customs for cultural sensitivity.

Health, Comfort, and Medical:

- [ ] Refillable water bottle.
- [ ] Diet-friendly snacks.
- [ ] Non-toxic sunblock.
- [ ] Natural insect repellent.
- [ ] Prescription medications.
- [ ] Copies of your prescriptions.

Apparel and Gear:

- [ ] Headlamp or flashlight with red light setting.
- [ ] Quick-drying, breathable clothing for varying temperatures:
    - 2-3 pairs of pants.
    - 2-3 pairs of shorts.
    - 3-4 short-sleeved shirts.
    - 1-2 hooded sweatshirt or light jacket.
    - Enough underwear and socks for each day.
    - Bathing suit.
- [ ] Footwear:
    - Sandals or flip flops.
    - Sneakers/walking shoes.
- [ ] Warm clothes for cooler nights.
- [ ] Hat, headscarf, and/or bandana or hair ties.
- [ ] Raincoat.
- [ ] Sunglasses

Toiletries and Accessories:

- [ ] Bathroom items: toothbrush, toothpaste, floss, shampoo, and soap (biodegradable only).

Items for the Altar:

- [ ] Personal memento or keepsake.

Personal Items:

- [ ] Journal, pen, and art supplies.
- [ ] Books for leisure reading.
- [ ] Travel alarm clock or watch.

If Bringing a Service Dog:

- [ ] Essential gear and documentation for the service dog.

Protective Measures:

- [ ] Waterproof bags for electronics and valuables.
- [ ] Trusted friend to travel with to reduce stress and danger.

What to Leave Behind:

- ☐ Valuables and sentimental items.
- ☐ Excess technology.
- ☐ Makeup and non-essential personal items.
- ☐ Alcohol, cannabis, and any non-prescribed medication.
- ☐ Weapons of any kind (including personal knife and/or multi-tool).

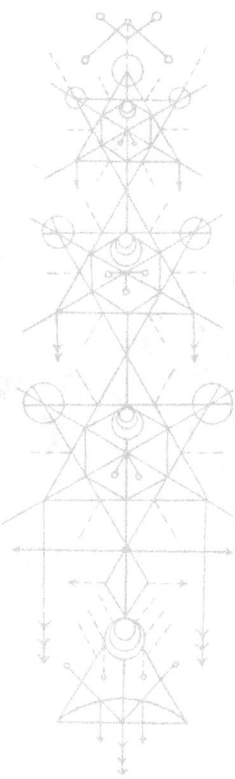

THE JOURNEY

"Life lived in the absence of the psychedelic experience that primordial shamanism is based on is life trivialized, life denied, life enslaved to the ego."

-Terence McKenna
Author

LETTING GO OF EXPECTATIONS

"Trust, Let Go, and Be Open"- Bill Richards, PhD

For those who've been through so much, learning to "let go of expectations" is a helpful piece of advice. This journey into psychedelics is different from any mission you've been on. It's about exploring the deep parts of your mind, a place where feelings and discoveries shape the path, not the physical world you're used to.

Understanding Intentions vs. Expectations:

It's important to know the difference between intentions and expectations before you start. Intentions are like your guideposts or goals for the journey. They're about what you hope to learn or heal without demanding a specific result. Expectations, though, are fixed ideas of how things should go, and they can lead to disappointment if things don't happen as planned. Much as in life, where adaptability and clear goals are key, set your intentions for your psychedelic journey clearly but let go of strict expectations about what will happen.

Embracing What Comes:

The first step is accepting that, even with preparation, you can't predict everything about your psychedelic journey.

Trust:

Trust is your foundation here. It includes faith in the process, confidence in your guide, healer, or therapist, and, most importantly, trust in yourself. Remember, you have the inner strength to face whatever comes your way, drawing on the same courage that has carried you through life's challenges.

Let Go:

Letting go means releasing your hold on what you think should happen, allowing the journey to happen naturally. It's about surrender, like finally exhaling a breath you've been holding. This mindset invites you to be open to all parts of the experience, from the challenging to the beautiful moments.

Be Open:

Being open means you're ready to accept whatever the experience brings with curiosity and without judging. It's about welcoming every moment with an open heart, ready to dive deep into yourself with kindness and an open mind.

During the Journey:

As you step into this experience, keep the idea of "Trust, Let Go, and Be Open" in your heart. Let these words guide you, showing you that the true journey of healing and discovery comes from letting go and allowing the experience to lead you.

JOURNEY TIPS FOR CEREMONIES

During the Ceremony:

Every individual's journey is unique, and there is no singular right or wrong way to engage with the ceremony. During the ceremony, it's essential to honor the uniqueness of your journey and the emotions that arise, whether they manifest as a flood of tears or bursts of laughter. The core principle is respect—both for your own process and the experiences of others. It is crucial to maintain personal space and allow others to navigate their experiences without interference.

Ceremony Dynamics:

Ceremonial gatherings typically begin with participants assembling in the designated space, where each individual may undergo a smudging or cleansing ritual led by a facilitator using elements like alcohol mist, tobacco smoke, or sage.

The ceremony officially starts with everyone seated, and a facilitator provides an overview, setting expectations for the journey ahead. After consuming the medicine (often referred to as a sacrament in ceremonial settings), participants are encouraged to lie down on their mats and may use eye masks designed to allow open-eyed darkness gazing. This, alongside the guided music and periods of silence that punctuate the ceremony, fosters deep introspection.

Support Availability:

Facilitators and sitters are present to ensure your safety and support your spiritual journey. While they may allow you to process deep emotions independently, they are always available for assistance—signal them by raising your hand or asking for help.

Hydration and Physical Needs:

Stay hydrated throughout the ceremony, and if you require assistance with water, don't hesitate to ask. Given the altered state of consciousness, tasks like walking may prove challenging. If you need to use the restroom, request a sitter's guidance. For safety, please do not lock the bathroom door.

Emotional Management:

Breathing deeply and focusing on each breath can help ground you during intense emotional states. Grounding exercises help here as well. Participants may express their energy in various forms, and facilitators typically allow these expressions to flow naturally. If you need reassurance or help, raising your hand or asking for help will quickly bring assistance.

Staying Within the Ceremony Space:

The collective energy and safety within the ceremonial circle are paramount. If you feel compelled to step outside, ask a sitter for accompaniment, maintaining the integrity and safety of the sacred space established for the journey.

GUIDELINES FOR CEREMONY PARTICIPATION

Participating in a ceremony comes with guidelines designed to honor the sacred space, the traditions involved, and the collective healing journey. Below are common rules anchored by the foundational principle of "Respect."

- **Respect the Sacraments:** Honor the sacred medicines and the ancestral traditions behind their use.

- **Practice Cultural Humility:** Everyone comes to this experience with diverse backgrounds and lived experiences. Please be mindful of your words, humor, and actions.

- **Follow Guidance:** Adhere to the instructions and guidelines provided by ceremony facilitators, musicians, and sitters.

- **Honor the Healing Process:** Recognize and respect your own healing journey and that of others, understanding that each participant's experience is deeply personal.

- **Maintain Personal Boundaries:** Be mindful of others' personal space and boundaries within the group setting.

- **Stay Present With Your Own Experience:** Allow facilitators to tend to fellow participants who may be struggling, as tempting as it may be to want to offer a helping hand!

- **Allow for Individual Experiences:** Acknowledge that everyone is on their unique spiritual path, deserving of their own judgment-free space, tranquility, and silence.

- **Manage Emotional Expression:** While expressing emotions like crying and laughing is encouraged, refrain from vocalizing or physically interacting with others during the ceremony to maintain a respectful and undisturbed environment for all.

- **Zero Tolerance for Harassment:** A strict policy against sexual harassment, gossiping, bullying, or violence is enforced to ensure the safety and respect of all participants and staff.

- **Prohibition of Sexual Activity:** Engaging in any form of sexual activity during the ceremony, including solitary acts or consensual activities between couples, is generally not allowed to preserve the integrity of the sacred space.

- **Maintain Confidentiality:** Please keep the experiences, words, and sharing of others confidential by not repeating/relaying outside of your retreat cohort. What happens on a retreat stays on retreat!

These guidelines are put in place to safeguard the sanctity of the ceremony, support each individual's healing process, and foster a respectful and harmonious communal experience.

GUIDELINES FOR PARTICIPATING IN NON-CEREMONIAL PSYCHEDELIC EXPERIENCES

Participation in any psychedelic experience demands respect for the process and those involved. Here are some guidelines to help ensure a respectful and safe experience:

1. **Respect the Process:** Honor the psychedelic and the intentions behind its use.
2. **Adherence to Guidance:** Follow any protocols or guidelines provided by the facilitators or therapists.
3. **Honor Individual Journeys:** Respect each person's unique path and healing process, understanding the deeply personal nature of psychedelic experiences.
4. **Personal Boundaries:** Keep a respectful distance and be mindful of personal space within the group or therapeutic setting.
5. **Focus on Your Experience:** Allow facilitators to manage the session and assist other participants as needed.
6. **Allow for Individual Expression:** Support the personal experiences of others by maintaining a quiet and supportive environment.
7. **Appropriate Emotional Expression:** Express emotions in a manner that respects the shared space and does not disrupt others.
8. **Zero Tolerance for Inappropriate Behavior:** Maintain a strict policy against harassment, ensuring a safe environment for all participants.
9. **Avoid Disruptive Activities:** Refrain from any activities that could distract from the sanctity of the experience, including excessive movement or noise.
10. **Confidentiality:** Respect the privacy of others by keeping shared experiences confidential within the group.

These guidelines help create a supportive and respectful environment, enabling all participants to engage deeply with their psychedelic experiences and fostering conditions conducive to profound personal growth and healing.

JOURNEY TIPS FOR OTHER PSYCHEDELIC SESSIONS

During the Experience: Every individual's journey with psychedelics is deeply personal and varies with each experience. Whether you are participating in a controlled therapeutic setting, a guided group session, or a carefully prepared personal setting, it's vital to approach the experience with an open heart and mind. Allow yourself to fully engage with the emotions and thoughts that arise, ensuring you honor your process and respect your boundaries.

Experience Dynamics: Each setting may begin differently but typically involves settling into a comfortable space prepared ahead of time, ensuring all needed items like water, snacks, and comfort items like blankets are within easy reach. In a therapeutic setting, the session might start with a discussion or set of guidelines provided by a therapist or guide. After ingesting the psychedelic, participants are often encouraged to use tools like eye masks or headphones to enhance introspection, supported by music or guided meditation audio. For people using ketamine, some providers are significantly more "medical" than others. Please make sure you ask your provider about what the experience will be like before signing up.

Support Availability: Whether in a clinical, group, or individual setting, support should be accessible. In therapeutic or guided experiences, professionals or trained sitters are available to ensure safety and provide support. They facilitate the session and are ready to assist if you signal or ask for help.

Hydration and Physical Needs: It's crucial to stay hydrated and comfortable throughout the experience. Assistance should be readily available for any physical needs, including help reaching the restroom. Movement might be impaired due to the psychedelic's effects, so it's safe to ask for assistance when needed.

Emotional Management: Managing intense emotions can be challenging. Techniques like deep breathing, focusing on tactile sensations, or even grounding exercises can help maintain a sense of calm. Expression of emotions is natural and should be allowed to flow as needed, but if overwhelmed, signal to a sitter or therapist for support.

Staying Within the Designated Space: Maintaining the integrity of the experience often requires staying within a designated safe area. If you need to leave the area for any reason, ensure to communicate with your guide, sitter or therapist to maintain safety and support throughout the session.

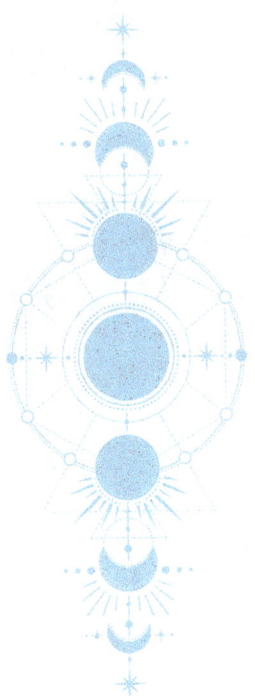

JOURNEY LOGS

Journey Log 1

DATE: /   /

Mindset going in:

_____

_____

_____

_____

Intensity Felt (1-5):

(1)   (2)   (3)   (4)   (5)

Medicine/Sacrament used:

_____

My intention for this journey was:

_____

_____

_____

_____

_____

_____

_____

_____

Which aspects of this journey stand out most? Were there memories, visual imagery, sensations, and/or emotions that you encountered?

_____

_____

_____

_____

_____

_____

_____

What was the essence of the message the medicine shared with you? Is there an aspect of your experience that feels profoundly transformed now?

_____

_____

_____

_____

_____

_____

_____

_____

_____

What elements of this journey were truly unforgettable, be they positive or negative? Were you surprised by anything? In which moments did you fully surrender, and when did you perceive yourself holding back?

_____

_____

_____

_____

_____

_____

_____

_____

_____

Were you called to undertake a specific action or change during your journey?

It is recommended that you wait at least two weeks before implementing any major conclusions you have reached to really make sure that these decisions are well-integrated and reflect a stable emotional state, rather than being impulsive reactions influenced by the immediate intensity of the experience. This period allows for thorough reflection, grounding, and consultation, enhancing the likelihood that any changes made are beneficial and sustainable.

What is one action you can take to keep this experience alive?

Journey Notes

Journey Notes

Journey Notes

Journey Notes

Journey Log 2

DATE: /   /

Mindset going in:

_____

_____

_____

Intensity Felt (1-5):

① ② ③ ④ ⑤

Medicine/Sacrament used:

_____

My intention for this journey was:

_____

_____

_____

_____

_____

_____

_____

Which aspects of this journey stand out most? Were there memories, visual imagery, sensations, and/or emotions that you encountered?

_____

_____

_____

_____

_____

_____

_____

_____

What was the essence of the message the medicine shared with you? Is there an aspect of your experience that feels profoundly transformed now?

_____

_____

_____

_____

_____

_____

_____

_____

_____

What elements of this journey were truly unforgettable, be they positive or negative? Were you surprised by anything? In which moments did you fully surrender, and when did you perceive yourself holding back?

_____

_____

_____

_____

_____

_____

_____

_____

_____

Were you called to undertake a specific action or change during your journey?

It is recommended that you wait at least two weeks before implementing any major conclusions you have reached to really make sure that these decisions are well-integrated and reflect a stable emotional state, rather than being impulsive reactions influenced by the immediate intensity of the experience. This period allows for thorough reflection, grounding, and consultation, enhancing the likelihood that any changes made are beneficial and sustainable.

What is one action you can take to keep this experience alive?

Journey Notes

Journey Notes

Journey Notes

Journey Notes

Journey Log 3

DATE: /   /

Mindset going in:

_____

_____

_____

Intensity Felt (1-5):

(1)   (2)   (3)   (4)   (5)

Medicine/Sacrament used:

_____

My intention for this journey was:

_____

_____

_____

_____

_____

_____

_____

_____

Which aspects of this journey stand out most? Were there memories, visual imagery, sensations, and/or emotions that you encountered?

_____

_____

_____

_____

_____

_____

_____

What was the essence of the message the medicine shared with you? Is there an aspect of your experience that feels profoundly transformed now?

_____

_____

_____

_____

_____

_____

_____

_____

_____

_____

What elements of this journey were truly unforgettable, be they positive or negative? Were you surprised by anything? In which moments did you fully surrender, and when did you perceive yourself holding back?

_____

_____

_____

_____

_____

_____

_____

_____

_____

_____

Were you called to undertake a specific action or change during your journey?

It is recommended that you wait at least two weeks before implementing any major conclusions you have reached to really make sure that these decisions are well-integrated and reflect a stable emotional state, rather than being impulsive reactions influenced by the immediate intensity of the experience. This period allows for thorough reflection, grounding, and consultation, enhancing the likelihood that any changes made are beneficial and sustainable.

What is one action you can take to keep this experience alive?

Journey Notes

Journey Notes

Journey Notes

Journey Notes

Journey Log 4

DATE: /   /

Mindset going in:

_____

_____

_____

Intensity Felt (1-5):

① ② ③ ④ ⑤

Medicine/Sacrament used:

_____

My intention for this journey was:

_____

_____

_____

_____

_____

_____

_____

Which aspects of this journey stand out most? Were there memories, visual imagery, sensations, and/or emotions that you encountered?

_____

_____

_____

_____

_____

_____

What was the essence of the message the medicine shared with you? Is there an aspect of your experience that feels profoundly transformed now?

_____

_____

_____

_____

_____

_____

_____

_____

_____

What elements of this journey were truly unforgettable, be they positive or negative? Were you surprised by anything? In which moments did you fully surrender, and when did you perceive yourself holding back?

_____

_____

_____

_____

_____

_____

_____

_____

Were you called to undertake a specific action or change during your journey?

It is recommended that you wait at least two weeks before implementing any major conclusions you have reached to really make sure that these decisions are well-integrated and reflect a stable emotional state, rather than being impulsive reactions influenced by the immediate intensity of the experience. This period allows for thorough reflection, grounding, and consultation, enhancing the likelihood that any changes made are beneficial and sustainable.

What is one action you can take to keep this experience alive?

Journey Notes

Journey Notes

Journey Notes

Journey Notes

INTEGRATION

"Psychedelics can act as catalysts for personal and spiritual growth, helping us to shed old patterns and beliefs, and embracing new ways of being that are more in alignment with our true selves."

-Rachel Harris, PhD
Psychologist and Author

WHAT IS PSYCHEDELIC INTEGRATION?

Psychedelics show us parts of ourselves and the universe that we don't usually see, offering new ways to understand life. It can break down old patterns, but it also means learning to live with a new kind of freedom, letting go of the strict rules we set for ourselves.

"Integration" means putting things together to make something complete, starting fresh. It comes from words that mean "to make whole" or "to put parts together." So, when we talk about integrating a psychedelic experience, we're talking about bringing together different parts of ourselves into a more united, complete person.

Connecting with others can help with integration. This could be talking to a therapist who knows about integration, joining a group, or just being with friends and family who get it. Spending time in nature or with animals can also help. Self-care, like writing in a journal, meditating, yoga, martial arts, painting, or gardening, can be really good during this time.

Taking some kind of action is also part of a transformative experience. If your journey brought up tough memories or something you need to work through, what steps do you need to take now? If you had a big realization or got inspired, what should you do about it? Using psychedelics responsibly means being ready to deal with whatever comes up and staying aware of what's happening inside and around you as you do this important inner work.

NAVIGATING INTEGRATION

The journey through a psychedelic experience can unfold across multiple dimensions of your being—physical, mental, emotional, relational, and spiritual. Each dimension may present its unique challenges and insights, necessitating a tailored approach to integration. Just as you've navigated various terrains in life, from physical demands to mental and emotional resilience, the integration process after a psychedelic journey mirrors this complexity, offering pathways to weave the insights gained into the fabric of your daily life.

Physical Integration:

For many, the psychedelic experience manifests physically, revealing the body's wisdom and, sometimes, its pain. To honor and support your body post-experience:

- **Stay an extra day (or three!):** If possible, reserve some free days after your retreat. An additional 1-3 days before returning to work or "real life" can significantly support your integration, allowing you to stay immersed in your process, continue self-care practices, and avoid rushing back into your usual pace of life. This extra time can be invaluable for easing the transition from your profound experience back to everyday reality.

- **Nourish and Hydrate:** Prioritize a clean diet rich in whole foods and stay well-hydrated. Your body has been through a profound experience; treat it with care.

- **Rest and Move:** To maintain physical harmony, balance restful practices like meditation and adequate sleep with gentle movement such as walking, yoga, or stretching.

- **Nature and Nurture:** Spend time in nature to reconnect with the earth's grounding energy. Consider bodywork or therapies like massage, sauna sessions, or cold showers to support physical healing further.

Mental Integration:

A psychedelic journey often sparks significant shifts in perception and understanding. To support these mental changes:

- **Cultivate Curiosity:** Learn new skills or read books that interest you. This is a time to feed your mind with growth and exploration.
- **Creative Expression:** Channel your insights into creative outlets—writing, painting, music—anything that allows you to express and explore the depths of your experience.
- **Mindful Environments:** Create spaces that inspire tranquility and reflection. Your surroundings can greatly influence your mental state and facilitate continued insight. Be careful with social media and news—try and avoid them for as long as you can.

Emotional Integration:

Emotional revelations during a psychedelic experience can be intense and revealing. To integrate these emotional shifts:

- **Gratitude Practice:** Start or end each day by noting aspects of your life for which you're grateful. This practice can shift perspectives and cultivate a positive emotional landscape.
- **Express and Release:** Journaling about your feelings or engaging in expressive arts can be therapeutic. Don't shy away from sharing your experiences with trusted friends or a therapist.
- **Compassion Meditation:** Practices like loving-kindness meditation can help you extend compassion to yourself and others, fostering emotional healing and connection. Pay extra attention to how you talk to yourself.

Relational Integration:

Psychedelic experiences often illuminate the importance of connections and relationships. To strengthen your relational world:

- **Deepen Connections:** Create opportunities for meaningful interactions with friends and family. These connections are vital for emotional support and understanding.
- **Rekindle and Resolve:** Reach out to old friends or address unresolved issues in current relationships. Honesty and vulnerability can open doors to deeper bonds.
- **Community Engagement:** Find and join communities that resonate with your interests or experiences. Shared passions can lead to meaningful relationships and support networks.

Spiritual Integration:

For those who touch upon the transcendent or confront existential questions during their journey, the path forward involves deep, personal exploration:

- **Spiritual Practices:** Whether it's meditation, prayer, or spending time in nature, find practices that connect you to something greater than yourself.
- **Sacred Studies:** If drawn to, explore sacred texts, spiritual teachings, or modern philosophies that resonate with your experience.
- **Mentorship and Community:** Seeking guidance from a mentor or joining a spiritual community can provide support and direction as you navigate your spiritual path.

Integration Timeline and Guidelines:

- **Be Patient:** Integration is a process that unfolds over weeks, months, or even years. Allow yourself the time and space to fully absorb and understand your experiences.
- **Gradual Re-entry:** Avoid making significant life decisions for at least two weeks following your psychedelic experience. Give yourself a period of reflection and grounding before taking significant steps.
- **Continued Exploration:** Regularly engage in practices and activities that support your integration. This could mean scheduled integration calls, continued journaling, or participation in supportive groups.

Remember, the true measure of a psychedelic journey lies not in the experience itself but in how you carry its lessons forward into your life. Like the multifaceted challenges faced during service, the path to integration requires adaptability, courage, and a commitment to self-discovery and growth.

INTEGRATION EXERCISES

The exercises that come next are to help you understand and grow from your psychedelic experience. Over the next four weeks, you will engage in a structured series of exercises, including:

1. **Embracing Change and Cultivating New Habits**
2. **New Sensations**
3. **Revisiting the Past**
4. **Envisioning The Future**

As part of that process, during this same period, you will also be asked to complete three exercises that work well together:

1. **Life Satisfaction Tracker**
2. **Developing New Habits**
3. **Personal Accountability Plan**

Take your time to think about each exercise. Read the questions and instructions carefully, then write down your thoughts and feelings. This can help you see patterns in your life that you might not have noticed before. Please pay attention to these patterns and let them teach you something new about yourself.

In addition to these structured exercises, making time for daily meditation is crucial. This practice will support your mental and emotional balance and help you process your experiences more deeply.

Maintaining a daily gratitude journal can help foster a positive outlook and recognize the transformative changes unfolding in your life. We have included a gratitude journal for you in this book.

If time permits, engage in creative play—activities that stimulate your imagination and provide a joyful, expressive outlet. These practices are not only enjoyable but reinforce the creative and flexible thinking enhanced by your psychedelic journey.

Remember, seeing the full benefits of working through these exercises might take a while. The changes you're making might be clear right away for some things, but for others, it might take months or even years. That's perfectly okay. Your friends and family might start to notice good changes in you too. Whether these changes happen fast or slowly, the important thing is to keep moving forward.

Think of psychedelic medicine as a spark that helps you change and grow. It's not the cure-all by itself. The exercises in this book are here to help you make the most of that spark, guiding you on your journey of transformation.

Week One Exercise: Embracing Change and Cultivating New Habits

Embarking on a journey of self-discovery and personal transformation often inspires a desire to ensure our external lives reflect our inner truths. For anyone seeking greater alignment in life, identifying and cultivating daily actions that resonate with core values is a powerful step forward. This first week is dedicated to exploring changes that feel authentic to you and laying the foundation for positive, meaningful habits. Through introspection and actionable steps, you'll begin to shape a life that mirrors your true self and supports growth and well-being.

Habits are the building blocks of our daily lives. They influence our actions, shape our routines, and ultimately determine our success and happiness. By focusing on creating positive habits, you can steer your life in the direction you desire, one small and intentional step at a time.

Reflecting on Your Life:

Before diving into habit formation, let's take a moment to reflect on areas of your life that may require adjustments to better align with who you truly are.

What aspects of your life currently feel out of sync with your true self? How do these misalignments affect your sense of balance and well-being?

Consider the values that are most important to you. In which areas of your life are you not living according to these values?

_____
_____
_____
_____
_____
_____
_____
_____
_____
_____

Which relationships no longer serve your growth, and where might clearer boundaries enhance your well-being?

_____
_____
_____
_____
_____
_____
_____
_____
_____
_____

Please complete the Habit Tracker exercise in the upcoming pages. Please update your Life Satisfaction Tracker with how you are feeling at the end of this week.

Week Two Exercise: New Sensations

Starting a path focused on health and feeling better can take a lot of time and effort. This week's activity is here to help you think about how you've been feeling lately.

Have you noticed any parts of your body feeling more open or accessible than before? Or maybe some parts where it feels like the "old you" is starting to fade away?

_____

_____

_____

_____

_____

_____

_____

_____

_____

_____

Have you started to feel curious about new hobbies or activities you hadn't thought about before?

_____

_____

_____

_____

_____

_____

_____

_____

_____

What new interests or thoughts have been on your mind recently?

_____

_____

_____

_____

_____

_____

_____

_____

_____

_____

Are there any new ways you've found to express yourself, or things you enjoy doing that feel right for you now?

_____

_____

_____

_____

_____

_____

_____

_____

_____

_____

Please complete the Habit Tracker exercise in the upcoming pages. Please update your Life Satisfaction Tracker with how you are feeling at the end of this week.

Week Three Exercise: Revisiting the Past

Psychedelic experiences can really help with going through tough memories in a way that feels safe and manageable. Sometimes, memories that used to make us feel stuck or that we might have tried to ignore can become clearer. This lets us face and deal with them more easily. Psychedelic journeys can be a strong way to look at, sort out, and lessen the impact of these hard memories.

Think about parts of your life where you can now say for sure, "That's behind me" and "I've moved on from that"?

_____

_____

_____

_____

_____

_____

_____

Do you notice any difference in how your body feels after recognizing this? How does this exercise make you feel? For some, spending a few minutes meditating on this can be helpful.

_____

_____

_____

_____

_____

Please complete the Habit Tracker exercise in the upcoming pages. Please update your Life Satisfaction Tracker with how you are feeling at the end of this week.

Week Four Exercise: Envisioning the Future

The big and moving experiences we have with psychedelics can really shake things up in our lives. These moments are special all on their own, but making real changes in our everyday lives based on what we've learned takes time and purposeful effort. It's an exciting time to explore what we're truly capable of and find out what makes us happiest.

What new opportunities do you see for yourself that seemed out of reach before?

What's changed inside you? If someone close to you had to point out what's different about you now, what would they say?

_____

_____

_____

_____

_____

_____

_____

_____

_____

How can you bring the lessons from your psychedelic experiences into your daily life?

_____

_____

_____

_____

_____

_____

_____

_____

_____

_____

_____

Who do you want to spend more time with? Are there any relationships or activities that aren't helping you grow?

_____
_____
_____
_____
_____
_____
_____
_____
_____
_____

What relationships or activities are not serving you?

_____
_____
_____
_____
_____
_____
_____
_____
_____
_____

Please complete the Habit Tracker exercise in the upcoming pages. Please update your Life Satisfaction Tracker with how you are feeling at the end of this week.

NEW EXERCISE: Please complete the "Personal Accountability Plan". This will help you with achieving your goals moving forward.

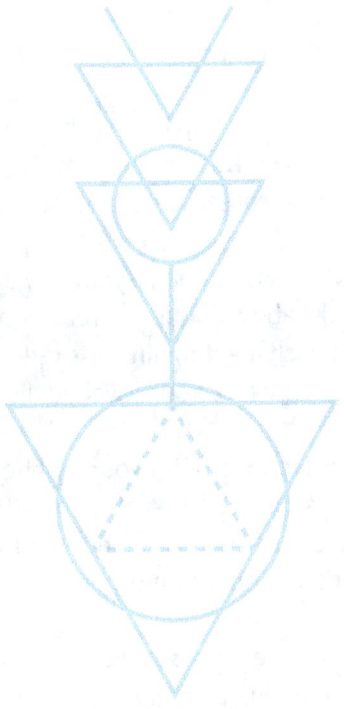

LIFE SATISFACTION TRACKER

Introduction to the Tracker:

The Life Satisfaction Tracker is designed as a simple tool to evaluate and improve your overall satisfaction with various life domains. By looking at your feelings across key areas of life, this tracker helps pinpoint both strengths and opportunities for growth. It offers a structured way to visualize changes in well-being over time, providing valuable insights into how different aspects of your life evolve in response to your psychedelic journey.

Instructions for Using the Tracker:

- **Assessment:** Before and after your psychedelic experience, rate your satisfaction in each area on a scale from 1 to 10, where 1 represents 'not satisfied at all' and 10 indicates 'completely satisfied'.

- **Pre-Psychedelic Reflections:** Before your psychedelic experience, take a moment to think about your current strengths and areas for improvement within each life domain. This reflection will help you focus your intentions and prepare for your psychedelic experience.

- **Post-Psychedelic Reflections:** After your psychedelic experience, reflect on any shifts in your satisfaction levels across the domains. This helps you identify the impact of the experience and areas that may require ongoing attention or additional support.

- **Identify Strengths and Weaknesses:** Use this tool to determine areas of strength and those requiring attention. This assessment will guide your focus before the experience and help you recognize both improvements and persisting challenges afterward.

Domains of Life Satisfaction:

- **Personal Growth:** This domain assesses your feelings of self-improvement and personal development. Are you learning new skills, overcoming personal challenges, and growing in self-awareness and self-compassion?

- **Relationships:** Evaluate the quality and depth of your interactions with family, friends, and colleagues. Are these relationships supportive, fulfilling, and nurturing?

- **Health and Well-Being:** This area covers both physical and mental health. Consider your overall health, fitness levels, dietary habits, and mental state.

- **Purpose and Contribution:** Reflect on your sense of purpose and the impact you have on the world. Are you engaged in activities that feel meaningful and contribute positively to others' lives?

Completing the Tracker:

Each week, after rating each domain, take a few minutes to reflect on the changes. Note any increases or decreases in your scores and consider what actions might enhance areas where satisfaction is lower. This ongoing process encourages a proactive approach to cultivating a balanced and fulfilling life.

Life Satisfaction Tracker

Instructions: Before and after your psychedelic experience, rate your satisfaction in each area on a scale from 1 to 10, where 1 represents 'not satisfied at all' and 10 indicates 'completely satisfied'.

Area of Satisfaction	Pre-Psychedelic	Week 1	Week 2	Week 3	Week 4
Personal Growth					
Relationships					
Health and Wellbeing					
Purpose and Contribution					

The following pages provide additional areas for reflection.

Pre-Psychedelic Reflections

Area of Satisfaction	Strengths	Areas of Improvement
Personal Growth		
Relationships		
Health and Wellbeing		
Purpose and Contribution		

Post Psychedelic Reflections

Area of Satisfaction	Strengths	Areas of Improvement
Personal Growth		
Relationships		
Health and Wellbeing		
Purpose and Contribution		

DEVELOPING NEW HABITS

As we venture into creating new habits, remember that small, consistent steps can lead to significant life changes. This section will guide you through selecting and forming habits that support your journey toward authenticity and fulfillment over a 4-week period.

Exercise: Creating New Habits

1. Identify Your Habits:
- Reflecting on your values and the areas of life you're focused on improving, identify three habits you believe will most positively impact your journey. What small daily actions can lead you toward your ideal self?

2. Define Clear Actions:
- For each habit, define a simple, specific action. How will this action look in your daily routine? Example: Instead of "be more active," choose "walk for 10 minutes every morning before breakfast."

3. Cue-Setting
- Determine a daily reminder for each habit. What consistent part of your routine can act as a cue to perform this new habit?

4. Make It Attractive:
- Find a way to make each habit appealing. This could be listening to your favorite podcast while exercising or treating yourself to a healthy smoothie afterward.

5. Start Small:
- Start with the smallest feasible step and gradually increase the difficulty. What is the minimum you can begin with that feels almost too easy?

6. Track Your Progress:
- Use the habit tracker for the next four weeks. Mark off each day you successfully perform your habit. Celebrate each day you follow through with your intentions.

7. Reflect and Adjust:
- At the end of the week, reflect on your experiences. What successes did you have? What challenges arose, and how can you adjust your approach to overcome them?

Remember, the journey of building new habits is a marathon, not a sprint. Be patient with yourself, and recognize that small, consistent actions lead to big changes over time. Use this 4-week challenge as a starting point to cultivate habits that will enrich your life and support your journey towards well-being.

Habit #1:

Habit 1: _____

- (Define your new habit in a statement. Example, "I will behavior at time in location")

Visual or Behavioral Cue: _____

- (Example, "Place a pull-up bar on your bedroom door")

Pair your new habit with an existing habit: _____

- (Example, "I will do pullups every time I walk through my bedroom door)

How will this be enticing and easy

- (Example: I will put my earbuds in and listen to my favorite music when doing pushups. I will start with X pullups per day and then ramp up.)

Habit #2:

Habit 2: _____

- (Define your new habit in a statement. Example, "I will behavior at time in location")

Visual or Behavioral Cue: _____

- (Example, "Place a pull-up bar on your bedroom door")

Pair your new habit with an existing habit: _____

- (Example, "I will do pullups every time I walk through my bedroom door)

How will this be enticing and easy

- (Example: I will put my earbuds in and listen to my favorite music when doing pushups. I will start with X pull-ups per day and then ramp up.)

Habit #3:

Habit 3: _____
- (Define your new habit in a statement. Example, "I will behavior at time in location")

Visual or Behavioral Cue: _____
- (Example, "Place a pull-up bar on your bedroom door")

Pair your new habit with an existing habit: _____
- (Example, "I will do pullups every time I walk through my bedroom door)

How will this be enticing and easy
- (Example: I will put my earbuds in and listen to my favorite music when doing pushups. I will start with X pull-ups per day and then ramp up.)

HABIT TRACKER

Week 1

HABIT	M	T	W	T	F	S	S

Week 2

HABIT	M	T	W	T	F	S	S

Week 3

HABIT	M	T	W	T	F	S	S

Week 4

HABIT	M	T	W	T	F	S	S

PERSONAL ACCOUNTABILITY PLAN

Congratulations on successfully tracking your habits and life satisfaction for the past 4 weeks! This Personal Accountability tool is designed to help you transition from initial tracking to setting and achieving long-term goals using the SMART (Specific, Measurable, Attainable, Relevant, Time-Bound) framework.

Instructions for Use:

First, create your goals:

- **Specific Goal Setting:** Clearly define your goal. Make it specific and straightforward, such as "Improve my physical fitness" or "Develop a daily meditation practice."

- **Measurable Progress:** Maintain a log to record your daily or weekly progress. This log should include activities related to your goal, milestones achieved, and any challenges encountered.

- **Action Steps:** Outline concrete steps you will take to reach your goal. Specify actions that are practical and within your ability to perform. For example, if your goal is to improve fitness, your action steps might be "Walk 30 minutes a day, three times a week."

- **Relevant:** Explain why this goal is important to you. Connecting your goal to your values or long-term objectives increases motivation and commitment.

- **Timeline:** Set a clear deadline or time frame for achieving your goal and for reviewing progress. This could be a few weeks, months, or a specific date.

Next, **TRACK** your progress. Maintain a log to record your daily or weekly progress. This log should include activities related to your goal, milestones achieved, and any challenges encountered. You can do this in the worksheet itself or in another place that is more suitable for your specific needs.

At the end of each review period, **REVIEW** what you've accomplished and what difficulties you've faced. Reflect on what you've learned and how you can improve moving forward.

Finally, make **ADJUSTMENTS** to your action steps or timeline based on your reflections. Adapting your plan based on real-world experiences is crucial for ongoing success and helps refine your approach.

By focusing on **SMART** goals, you can create a structured and effective plan that guides your actions and helps measure your progress, ensuring that you continue to grow and improve beyond the initial 30-day tracking period.

Remember, the key to this exercise is consistency and honesty with yourself. Regular check-ins and adjustments are part of the process and critical to developing personal accountability and achieving your goals.

Personal Accountability Worksheet   Date:

S	M	A
Specific Clearly define your goal.	**Measurable** How will you measure your success?	**Achievable** How will you achieve this goal?

1		Qty:_____ Date:_____ Qty:_____ Date:_____ Qty:_____ Date:_____	Step1: Step2: Step3:
2		Qty:_____ Date:_____ Qty:_____ Date:_____ Qty:_____ Date:_____	Step1: Step2: Step3:
3		Qty:_____ Date:_____ Qty:_____ Date:_____ Qty:_____ Date:_____	Step1: Step2: Step3:
4		Qty:_____ Date:_____ Qty:_____ Date:_____ Qty:_____ Date:_____	Step1: Step2: Step3:
5		Qty:_____ Date:_____ Qty:_____ Date:_____ Qty:_____ Date:_____	Step1: Step2: Step3:

R	T
Relevant	**Timebound**
Why is this goal important to you?	When will you achieve this goal by?

GRATITUDE JOURNALS

"How long will this last, this delicious feeling of being alive, of having penetrated the veil which hides beauty and the wonders of celestial vistas? It doesn't matter, as there can be nothing but gratitude for even a glimpse of what exists for those who can become open to it."

-Alexander "Sasha" Shulgin, Ph.D.
Chemist, biochemist, pharmacologist, psychopharmacologist, and author

Daily Gratitude Journal

/   /

The root of joy is gratefulness.
- David Steindl-Rast

HOW DO I FEEL RIGHT NOW?

THREE THINGS I AM GRATEFUL FOR AND WHY:

1 _____
2 _____
3 _____

THREE GOOD THINGS THAT HAPPENED TODAY:

1 _____
2 _____
3 _____

HOW COULD I HAVE MADE TODAY BETTER?

_____
_____
_____

FREE FLOW THOUGHTS/NOTES FROM TODAY:

_____
_____
_____
_____

Daily Gratitude Journal

/ /

We suffer more often from imagination than from reality.
- Seneca

HOW DO I FEEL RIGHT NOW?

THREE THINGS I AM GRATEFUL FOR AND WHY:

1 _____
2 _____
3 _____

THREE GOOD THINGS THAT HAPPENED TODAY:

1 _____
2 _____
3 _____

HOW COULD I HAVE MADE TODAY BETTER?

_____
_____
_____

FREE FLOW THOUGHTS/NOTES FROM TODAY:

_____
_____
_____
_____

Daily Gratitude Journal

/   /

A flower does not think of competing with the flower next to it.
It just blooms.

- Zen Shin

HOW DO I FEEL RIGHT NOW?

THREE THINGS I AM GRATEFUL FOR AND WHY:

1 _____

2 _____

3 _____

THREE GOOD THINGS THAT HAPPENED TODAY:

1 _____

2 _____

3 _____

HOW COULD I HAVE MADE TODAY BETTER?

_____

_____

_____

_____

FREE FLOW THOUGHTS/NOTES FROM TODAY:

_____

_____

_____

_____

Daily Gratitude Journal

/ /

What you think you become.
- Gautama Buddha

HOW DO I FEEL RIGHT NOW?

THREE THINGS I AM GRATEFUL FOR AND WHY:

1 _____
2 _____
3 _____

THREE GOOD THINGS THAT HAPPENED TODAY:

1 _____
2 _____
3 _____

HOW COULD I HAVE MADE TODAY BETTER?

_____
_____
_____

FREE FLOW THOUGHTS/NOTES FROM TODAY:

_____
_____
_____

Daily Gratitude Journal

/   /

A grateful mind is a great mind which
eventually attracts to itself great things.
- Plato

HOW DO I FEEL RIGHT NOW?

THREE THINGS I AM GRATEFUL FOR AND WHY:

1 _____
2 _____
3 _____

THREE GOOD THINGS THAT HAPPENED TODAY:

1 _____
2 _____
3 _____

HOW COULD I HAVE MADE TODAY BETTER?

_____
_____
_____

FREE FLOW THOUGHTS/NOTES FROM TODAY:

_____
_____
_____
_____

Daily Gratitude Journal

/   /

It is not how much we do, but how much love we put into doing.
- Mother Teresa

HOW DO I FEEL RIGHT NOW?

THREE THINGS I AM GRATEFUL FOR AND WHY:

1 _____
2 _____
3 _____

THREE GOOD THINGS THAT HAPPENED TODAY:

1 _____
2 _____
3 _____

HOW COULD I HAVE MADE TODAY BETTER?

_____

_____

_____

FREE FLOW THOUGHTS/NOTES FROM TODAY:

_____

_____

_____

Daily Gratitude Journal

/ /

Our life is what our thoughts make it.
- Marcus Aurelius

HOW DO I FEEL RIGHT NOW?

THREE THINGS I AM GRATEFUL FOR AND WHY:

1 _____

2 _____

3 _____

THREE GOOD THINGS THAT HAPPENED TODAY:

1 _____

2 _____

3 _____

HOW COULD I HAVE MADE TODAY BETTER?

_____

_____

_____

FREE FLOW THOUGHTS/NOTES FROM TODAY:

_____

_____

_____

Daily Gratitude Journal

/   /

*Be careful how you are talking to yourself
because you are listening.*

- Lisa M Hayes

HOW DO I FEEL RIGHT NOW?

THREE THINGS I AM GRATEFUL FOR AND WHY:

1 _____

2 _____

3 _____

THREE GOOD THINGS THAT HAPPENED TODAY:

1 _____

2 _____

3 _____

HOW COULD I HAVE MADE TODAY BETTER?

FREE FLOW THOUGHTS/NOTES FROM TODAY:

Daily Gratitude Journal

/   /

Join with those who sing songs, tell stories, enjoy life...
because happiness is contagious.

- Paulo Coelho

HOW DO I FEEL RIGHT NOW?

THREE THINGS I AM GRATEFUL FOR AND WHY:

1 _____
2 _____
3 _____

THREE GOOD THINGS THAT HAPPENED TODAY:

1 _____
2 _____
3 _____

HOW COULD I HAVE MADE TODAY BETTER?

_____
_____
_____

FREE FLOW THOUGHTS/NOTES FROM TODAY:

_____
_____
_____

Daily Gratitude Journal

/ /

Part of being optimistic is keeping one's head pointed toward the sun, one's feet moving forward.

- Nelson Mandela

HOW DO I FEEL RIGHT NOW?

THREE THINGS I AM GRATEFUL FOR AND WHY:

1 _____
2 _____
3 _____

THREE GOOD THINGS THAT HAPPENED TODAY:

1 _____
2 _____
3 _____

HOW COULD I HAVE MADE TODAY BETTER?

_____
_____
_____

FREE FLOW THOUGHTS/NOTES FROM TODAY:

_____
_____
_____
_____

Daily Gratitude Journal

/   /

Be happy for this moment. This moment is your life.
- Omar Khayyam

HOW DO I FEEL RIGHT NOW?

THREE THINGS I AM GRATEFUL FOR AND WHY:

1 _____

2 _____

3 _____

THREE GOOD THINGS THAT HAPPENED TODAY:

1 _____

2 _____

3 _____

HOW COULD I HAVE MADE TODAY BETTER?

_____

_____

_____

FREE FLOW THOUGHTS/NOTES FROM TODAY:

_____

_____

_____

Daily Gratitude Journal

/   /

Gratitude will shift you to a higher frequency and you will attract much better things.
- Rhonda Byrne

HOW DO I FEEL RIGHT NOW?

THREE THINGS I AM GRATEFUL FOR AND WHY:

1 _____

2 _____

3 _____

THREE GOOD THINGS THAT HAPPENED TODAY:

1 _____

2 _____

3 _____

HOW COULD I HAVE MADE TODAY BETTER?

_____

_____

_____

FREE FLOW THOUGHTS/NOTES FROM TODAY:

_____

_____

_____

Daily Gratitude Journal

/   /

*Just one small positive thought in the morning
can change your whole day.*
- Dalai Lama

HOW DO I FEEL RIGHT NOW?

THREE THINGS I AM GRATEFUL FOR AND WHY:

1 _____

2 _____

3 _____

THREE GOOD THINGS THAT HAPPENED TODAY:

1 _____

2 _____

3 _____

HOW COULD I HAVE MADE TODAY BETTER?

_____

_____

_____

FREE FLOW THOUGHTS/NOTES FROM TODAY:

_____

_____

_____

Daily Gratitude Journal

/ /

Be here, now.
- Ram Dass

HOW DO I FEEL RIGHT NOW?

THREE THINGS I AM GRATEFUL FOR AND WHY:

1 _____

2 _____

3 _____

THREE GOOD THINGS THAT HAPPENED TODAY:

1 _____

2 _____

3 _____

HOW COULD I HAVE MADE TODAY BETTER?

_____

_____

_____

FREE FLOW THOUGHTS/NOTES FROM TODAY:

_____

_____

_____

_____

Daily Gratitude Journal

/ /

Everything will be ok in the end.
If it's not okay, it's not the end.
- John Lennon

HOW DO I FEEL RIGHT NOW?

THREE THINGS I AM GRATEFUL FOR AND WHY:

1 _____
2 _____
3 _____

THREE GOOD THINGS THAT HAPPENED TODAY:

1 _____
2 _____
3 _____

HOW COULD I HAVE MADE TODAY BETTER?

_____
_____
_____

FREE FLOW THOUGHTS/NOTES FROM TODAY:

_____
_____

Daily Gratitude Journal

/   /

Knowing others is intelligence;
knowing yourself is true wisdom
- Lao Tzu

HOW DO I FEEL RIGHT NOW?

THREE THINGS I AM GRATEFUL FOR AND WHY:

1 _____
2 _____
3 _____

THREE GOOD THINGS THAT HAPPENED TODAY:

1 _____
2 _____
3 _____

HOW COULD I HAVE MADE TODAY BETTER?

_____
_____
_____
_____

FREE FLOW THOUGHTS/NOTES FROM TODAY:

_____
_____
_____
_____

Daily Gratitude Journal

/   /

There is nothing either good or bad,
but thinking makes it so.
- William Shakespeare

HOW DO I FEEL RIGHT NOW?

THREE THINGS I AM GRATEFUL FOR AND WHY:

1 _____

2 _____

3 _____

THREE GOOD THINGS THAT HAPPENED TODAY:

1 _____

2 _____

3 _____

HOW COULD I HAVE MADE TODAY BETTER?

_____

_____

_____

FREE FLOW THOUGHTS/NOTES FROM TODAY:

_____

_____

_____

_____

Daily Gratitude Journal

/   /

Happiness is an inside job.
- William Arthur Ward

HOW DO I FEEL RIGHT NOW?

THREE THINGS I AM GRATEFUL FOR AND WHY:

1 _____
2 _____
3 _____

THREE GOOD THINGS THAT HAPPENED TODAY:

1 _____
2 _____
3 _____

HOW COULD I HAVE MADE TODAY BETTER?

_____
_____
_____

FREE FLOW THOUGHTS/NOTES FROM TODAY:

_____
_____
_____
_____

Daily Gratitude Journal

/   /

If you can change your mind, you can change your life.
- William James

HOW DO I FEEL RIGHT NOW?

THREE THINGS I AM GRATEFUL FOR AND WHY:

1 _____
2 _____
3 _____

THREE GOOD THINGS THAT HAPPENED TODAY:

1 _____
2 _____
3 _____

HOW COULD I HAVE MADE TODAY BETTER?

_____
_____
_____

FREE FLOW THOUGHTS/NOTES FROM TODAY:

_____
_____
_____

Daily Gratitude Journal

/   /

Let gratitude be the pillow upon
which you kneel to say your nightly prayer.

- Maya Angelou

HOW DO I FEEL RIGHT NOW?

THREE THINGS I AM GRATEFUL FOR AND WHY:

1 _____
2 _____
3 _____

THREE GOOD THINGS THAT HAPPENED TODAY:

1 _____
2 _____
3 _____

HOW COULD I HAVE MADE TODAY BETTER?

_____
_____
_____

FREE FLOW THOUGHTS/NOTES FROM TODAY:

_____
_____
_____
_____

Daily Gratitude Journal

/   /

This moment is all there is.
- Rumi

HOW DO I FEEL RIGHT NOW?

THREE THINGS I AM GRATEFUL FOR AND WHY:

1 _____

2 _____

3 _____

THREE GOOD THINGS THAT HAPPENED TODAY:

1 _____

2 _____

3 _____

HOW COULD I HAVE MADE TODAY BETTER?

_____

_____

_____

FREE FLOW THOUGHTS/NOTES FROM TODAY:

_____

_____

_____

Daily Gratitude Journal

/   /

You are what you repeatedly do.
- Aristotle

HOW DO I FEEL RIGHT NOW?

THREE THINGS I AM GRATEFUL FOR AND WHY:

1 _____
2 _____
3 _____

THREE GOOD THINGS THAT HAPPENED TODAY:

1 _____
2 _____
3 _____

HOW COULD I HAVE MADE TODAY BETTER?

_____
_____
_____
_____

FREE FLOW THOUGHTS/NOTES FROM TODAY:

_____
_____
_____
_____

Daily Gratitude Journal

/ /

You can't stop the waves, but you can learn to surf.
- Jon Kabat-Zinn

HOW DO I FEEL RIGHT NOW?

THREE THINGS I AM GRATEFUL FOR AND WHY:

1 _____
2 _____
3 _____

THREE GOOD THINGS THAT HAPPENED TODAY:

1 _____
2 _____
3 _____

HOW COULD I HAVE MADE TODAY BETTER?

_____
_____
_____

FREE FLOW THOUGHTS/NOTES FROM TODAY:

_____
_____
_____

Daily Gratitude Journal

/ /

Life wastes itself while we are preparing to live.
- Emerson

HOW DO I FEEL RIGHT NOW?

THREE THINGS I AM GRATEFUL FOR AND WHY:

1
2
3

THREE GOOD THINGS THAT HAPPENED TODAY:

1
2
3

HOW COULD I HAVE MADE TODAY BETTER?

FREE FLOW THOUGHTS/NOTES FROM TODAY:

Daily Gratitude Journal

/ /

The more grateful I am, the more beauty I see.
- Mary Davis

HOW DO I FEEL RIGHT NOW?

THREE THINGS I AM GRATEFUL FOR AND WHY:

1 _____
2 _____
3 _____

THREE GOOD THINGS THAT HAPPENED TODAY:

1 _____
2 _____
3 _____

HOW COULD I HAVE MADE TODAY BETTER?

_____
_____
_____

FREE FLOW THOUGHTS/NOTES FROM TODAY:

_____
_____
_____

Daily Gratitude Journal

/   /

Thoughts become things... choose the good ones!
- Mike Dooley

HOW DO I FEEL RIGHT NOW?

THREE THINGS I AM GRATEFUL FOR AND WHY:

1 _____
2 _____
3 _____

THREE GOOD THINGS THAT HAPPENED TODAY:

1 _____
2 _____
3 _____

HOW COULD I HAVE MADE TODAY BETTER?

_____
_____
_____

FREE FLOW THOUGHTS/NOTES FROM TODAY:

_____
_____
_____

Daily Gratitude Journal

/   /

You will never find rainbows, if you are looking down...
- Charlie Chaplin

HOW DO I FEEL RIGHT NOW?

THREE THINGS I AM GRATEFUL FOR AND WHY:

1 _____
2 _____
3 _____

THREE GOOD THINGS THAT HAPPENED TODAY:

1 _____
2 _____
3 _____

HOW COULD I HAVE MADE TODAY BETTER?

_____
_____
_____

FREE FLOW THOUGHTS/NOTES FROM TODAY:

_____
_____

Daily Gratitude Journal

/   /

Happiness is when what you think, what you say,
and what you do are in harmony.
- Mahatma Ghandi

HOW DO I FEEL RIGHT NOW?

THREE THINGS I AM GRATEFUL FOR AND WHY:

1 _____
2 _____
3 _____

THREE GOOD THINGS THAT HAPPENED TODAY:

1 _____
2 _____
3 _____

HOW COULD I HAVE MADE TODAY BETTER?

_____
_____
_____

FREE FLOW THOUGHTS/NOTES FROM TODAY:

_____
_____
_____
_____

Daily Gratitude Journal

/ /

If you want to be happy, be.

\- Leo Tolstoy

HOW DO I FEEL RIGHT NOW?

THREE THINGS I AM GRATEFUL FOR AND WHY:

1 _____

2 _____

3 _____

THREE GOOD THINGS THAT HAPPENED TODAY:

1 _____

2 _____

3 _____

HOW COULD I HAVE MADE TODAY BETTER?

_____

_____

_____

FREE FLOW THOUGHTS/NOTES FROM TODAY:

_____

_____

_____

CREATIVE PLAY

"Through our eyes, the universe is perceiving itself. Through our ears, the universe is listening to its harmonies. We are the witnesses through which the universe becomes conscious of its glory, of its magnificence.

-Alan Watts
Writer

COLORING

Coloring is like a quiet escape from the busy world around us. It's a calm activity that helps ease stress and lets us focus on how we're feeling inside. When you color, you stay in the here and now, fully noticing and enjoying the beauty of the picture you're working on. This activity is a great way to practice mindfulness.

The coloring pages in this part of the workbook are a perfect place for you to chill out, pay attention, and get creative. The detailed designs invite you into a world of colors and shapes, creating a peaceful spot where you can just be in the moment.

NOTEBOOK

As you step into the healing journey with psychedelics, you bring along your rich stories, lessons learned, and some questions looking for answers. The next pages are yours to fill—they're a space made just for you to write down, think through, and reflect on all that's on your mind as you get ready for what's coming.

Here, you can write about what scares you, what you hope for, what you're unsure about, and what you know for sure. No idea is too small; no feeling is too light. This is your safe place. Let your words come out freely, without holding back.

Writing in this journal is more than just getting ready; it's about taking back control—your story, your voice, your strength—as you stand ready to change and grow.

CONCLUDING
THOUGHTS

"For working purposes, you might separate the personal, the community and the planet, but within the vision, the cosmology of Indigenous communities of the Amazon rainforest, you do not separate the individual from the community from the planet, that's fictitious. Individual health is collective health, collective health includes the territory. We're talking about one ecosystem which is inseparable and it's very important to view it as one.

-Miguel Evanjuanoy
Inga from Colombia, engineer, and member of UMIYAC (the Union of Indigenous Medics and Yageceros of Colombia)

A NEW PATH

After exploring your inner world, absorbing the wisdom of your psychedelic journey, and using this workbook to transform, it's key to remember that awakening is a journey that keeps unfolding.

This path is both personal and shared. It's about building ties with others who get the shift from serving to discovering yourself. They offer the support and connection you might be looking for. Find groups or communities that match your vibe because they can be a big part of your healing journey.

Be careful about what you let into your life, from what you eat to the thoughts you entertain to what you watch. These choices shape your day-to-day life, helping you live in a way that's true to who you are.

As you bring the lessons from your psychedelic experiences into your regular life, look for ways to connect more deeply with people. It's through real connections that we can show the love inside us, hoping to make a world filled with compassion and unity.

Go back to this workbook now and then to remember the deep experiences that have shaped you and to keep the spark of change alive in your heart. Reflecting regularly helps us stay true to ourselves, ensuring that the insights we've gained keep guiding us.

Through your journey with psychedelics, may you deeply understand that you are enough, loved, and full of wisdom ready to be shared. May you feel a strong connection to something greater and trust yourself to make the right choices.

You are enough. You are worthy. You are loved.

RESOURCES

- For a life-threatening medical or mental health emergency, call **911** or go to your **nearest emergency room.**

Psychedelic Integration Support

- **Being True To You:** an online transformational and integration coaching company that provides psychedelic integration, general life coaching, and trains aspiring coaches. **beingtruetoyou.com**

- **Fireside Project:** Offers a 24/7 hotline that is available to support individuals experiencing a difficult psychedelic experience or seeking support for integrating psychedelic experiences. They do provide veteran-specific support **www.firesideproject.org**

- **MAPS psychedelic integration list** - This directory features individuals and organizations in the mental health field who help people integrate past psychedelic experiences. (These practitioners do NOT facilitate actual ceremonies.) There likely will be a fee for the providers' services, but we always encourage you to ask about sliding scale/military discount options. **integration.maps.org**

- **Psychedelic Support:** Provides psychedelic resources along with a directory of psychedelic-friendly therapists and psychedelic clinical trials seeking participants. **www.psychedelic.support**

Psychedelic Education

- **Clinical Trials:** Use this website to research clinical trials that may be available for you. **https://clinicaltrials.gov/**

- **Fluence:** A leading provider of continuing education in psychedelic integration and psychedelic-assisted therapy, committed to serving practitioners with evidence-based training and support. **www.fluencetraining.com**

- **Microdosing Collective:** Provides education and research on microdosing for optimal well-being. **www.microdosingcollective.org**

- **Psychedelic Support:** Provides free and comprehensive online courses and training from leaders in the psychedelic field for healthcare providers or those who are psychedelic curious. **www.psychedelic.support**

- **Psychedelics Today:** Provides resources, content, and education related to all things psychedelics, including their Vital Psychedelic Training. **www.psychedelicstoday.com**

- **Third Wave:** Dedicated to fostering the psychedelic movement by offering research-driven education, connecting individuals with trusted providers, and cultivating a global community for sharing and support. **thethirdwave.co**

Veteran Clinical Support

- **Beckley Foundation:** Besides offering fully funded programs for U.S. Veterans, the Beckley Foundation is involved in veteran suicide prevention research, in collaboration with the Heroic Hearts Project and Imperial College London, to study the efficacy of psychedelic-assisted therapies against veteran suicide. **www.beckleyretreats.com**

- **Cohen Veterans Network:** Provides in-person and virtual mental health services and case management to post-9/11 veterans. They also offer marriage counseling, relationship counseling, and help with children's behavioral issues. **www.cohenveteransnetwork.org**

- **Road Home Program:** Provides both inpatient and outpatient therapy, support, and resources for Military Sexual Trauma (MST) at no cost to the survivor. Treatment length varies. **roadhomeprogram.org**

- **Sunstone Therapies**: At the forefront of advancing the delivery of psychedelic-assisted therapy in the medical setting, focusing on clinical trials and committed to treating the whole person. **www.sunstonetherapies.com**

- **The Headstrong Project**: Established by veterans in 2012, provides confidential, barrier-free, and stigma-free PTSD treatment to servicemembers, veterans, and their families. The Headstrong Project provides up to 30 cost-free sessions as a part of their program, with additional low-cost support available. **www.theheadstrongproject.org**

- **The United States Department of Veterans Affairs (VA):** A resource for veterans, providing a wide range of services, including healthcare, disability compensation, vocational rehabilitation, education assistance, and more, across its extensive network of facilities. Notably, the VA operates under a structure where each VA medical center and clinic functions with a degree of independence, allowing them to tailor services to meet the specific needs of their local veteran community. Veterans are encouraged to connect directly with their local VA facility to understand the specific resources and support available. **www.va.gov/find-locations**

- **Warriors Heart:** Warriors Heart® provides private treatment to adult men and women 18 and older who are seeking inpatient treatment for chemical dependency, alcohol abuse, and co-occurring psychological disorders relating to PTSD (post-traumatic stress disorder) or the psychological effects of MTBI (mild traumatic brain injury). **www.warriorsheart.com**

Veteran and First Responder Nonprofits

- **Heroic Hearts Project:** A groundbreaking organization that helps veterans and their families overcome the impacts of PTSD and other military trauma through access to psychedelic programs alongside professional coaching, peer support, and a wealth of empowering resources. HHP has branches in the US, UK, Canada, and Australia. **www.heroicheartsproject.org**

- **The Hope Project:** An HHP Program that offers a lifeline for spouses affected by their partners' military service-related trauma, offering psychedelic retreats, education, personalized coaching, and a nurturing community to promote healing. It extends comprehensive programs to Veteran spouses and families as well as Gold Star wives. **www.thehope-project.org**

- **Healing Our Heroes:** Provides accessible and affordable mental health and legal psychedelic retreats to our veterans, first responders, retired CIA and FBI personnel, medical professionals, and others who have selflessly served and sacrificed for our communities. **www.healingourheroesflorida.org**

- **Illuminating Future Foundation:** A nonprofit committed to creating a world free from suicide by empowering, enlightening, and transforming the lives of veterans, first responders, and Gold/White Star Families through religious access to entheogenic medicine ceremonies. **www.theilluminating.co/illuminating-heroes**

- **Illuminating Future Foundation:** A nonprofit committed to creating a world free from suicide by empowering, enlightening, and transforming the lives of veterans, first responders, and Gold/White Star Families through religious access to entheogenic medicine ceremonies. **www.theilluminating.co/illuminating-heroes**

- **LEAP:** The Law Enforcement Action Partnership is an international 501(c)(3) nonprofit organization of criminal justice professionals advocating for drug policy and criminal justice reforms that will make communities safer. **lawenforcementactionpartnership.org**

- **Mission Within Foundation:** Since 2017, nearly 1,000 special operations veterans and their spouses have found relief from PTSD, mTBI, depression, and anxiety through their programs, with a significant portion overcoming PTSD diagnostic criteria. The Mission Within is also a voice for changing veteran narratives around psychedelic treatments. **www.missionwithin.org**

- **No Fallen Heroes:** An organization that believes sacred plant medicines can provide healing for mTBI, PTS, depression and anxiety. They partner with a number of organizations to help veterans, their families and first-responders to find healing solutions. **nofallenheroesfoundation.org**

- **S.I.R.E.N.:** "Supporting Initial Responders with Entheogenic Networking" was founded by experienced firefighters, addressing the critical mental health needs of first responders by advocating for and providing access to alternative therapies, including psychedelics. **thesirenproject.org**

- **VETS (Veterans Exploring Treatment Solutions):** Specializing in offering grants, coaching, and resources, VETS facilitates veterans and their spouses' access to psychedelic-assisted treatments in legal yet unregulated regions. Treatments cover a range of therapies, including iboga/ibogaine, ketamine, psilocybin, MDMA, 5-MeO-DMT, and ayahuasca. **www.vetssolutions.org**

ACKNOWLEDGMENTS

Special thanks to Jesse Gould, Jared Rinehart, and the Heroic Hearts Project team for their thoughts and suggestions as to how to make the content in this book more meaningful.

Thanks go to Lucy Martinez for your exceptional marketing support and friendship.

Heartfelt thanks go to Shana, Tom, Cal, and my extended family. I am also deeply grateful for the incredible spiritual community that I belong to in North Carolina, and to Lexie, Bill, and Wesley's leadership. Special appreciation and gratitude goes to Melissa, Alex, and Cole, as well as to New Leaf Collective, Corey 'Nav' Chase, and John Breckenridge, whose wisdom and guidance have profoundly shaped my path.

This journey towards healing and understanding would not be possible without the collective effort, passion, and courage of everyone mentioned and those unnamed who share and support our vision.

A GOOD PLACE FOR A DONATION: HEROIC HEARTS PROJECT

Looking for a place to make a difference? Heroic Hearts Project (HHP) is a non-profit organization dedicated to supporting veterans and their families in overcoming the impacts of PTSD and military trauma. By facilitating access to innovative psychedelic programs and providing comprehensive support resources, HHP fosters healing and personal growth within the veteran community. Established in 2017, HHP not only focuses on the direct care of veterans but also actively contributes to research and advocacy to expand access to these transformative treatment options. HHP aims to bring psychedelic healing for veterans home to the USA at scale.

The origins of HHP trace back to the profound personal journey of its founder, Jesse Gould, a former Army Ranger whose battle with severe PTSD led him to seek healing beyond traditional methods. His transformative experience at an ayahuasca retreat in the Peruvian jungle provided not just relief but a new direction in life. Moved by his own recovery, Jesse was compelled to create a pathway for his fellow veterans to find similar healing.

"Before Heroic Hearts, I was at my lowest point, feeling disconnected and hopeless. As my own pain began to lift, I knew I couldn't keep this journey to myself. I feel extremely fortunate that I found a safe psychedelic retreat in my time of need. But I also had to approach it without support. HHP is not about subjecting veterans to yet another treatment for their symptoms. It's about empowering veterans and their loved ones to embark on real, transformative experiences and to take their healing into their own hands. It's about ensuring that no one in this community feels alone or unsupported as they begin the deep work of unpacking trauma and reclaiming inner peace. This is not just my mission—it's a call to action for the healing, understanding, and compassion that everyone in the military community deserves."

Looking ahead, HHP is committed to expanding its reach and deepening its impact. The organization continues to sit at the forefront of the integration of psychedelic healthcare for veterans into mainstream acceptance and envisions a future where every veteran has access to the tools needed for substantial and sustainable healing.

www.heroicheartsproject.org

A GOOD PLACE FOR A DONATION: CHACRUNA

Want to support reciprocity in the psychedelic community, and support the protection of sacred plants and cultural traditions? The Chacruna Institute for Psychedelic Plant Medicines, founded by Brazilian anthropologist Dr. Bia Labate and American psychologist Dr. Clancy Cavnar, is dedicated to advancing public knowledge and acceptance of plant medicines and psychedelics.

Through high-quality research and educational initiatives, Chacruna works to destigmatize these substances and make academic knowledge accessible to a broader audience. The Institute serves as a bridge, connecting traditional ceremonial uses of plant medicines with the growing field of psychedelic science, enriching clinical and therapeutic settings with insights from the social sciences.

The Indigenous Reciprocity Initiative of the Americas (IRI) is a community-driven program led by Indigenous people to support biocultural conservation across the Americas. IRI unites 38 Indigenous groups from 20 partner organizations working on projects in food and water security, agroforestry, environmental health, land rights, and economic and educational empowerment. Each initiative is designed and implemented by the communities themselves, ensuring that all efforts are self-determined, aligned with local priorities, and never imposed from outside.

Through an approach based on reciprocity, IRI supports the evolving needs of these community-led projects, providing both financial aid and a collaborative platform to co-create educational resources. In its first year, with generous support like yours, IRI has raised over $165,000, empowering Indigenous organizations in their vital work to protect their land, culture, and environment.

www.chacruna.net

ABOUT THE CLINICAL REVIEWER

Meet Ken Weingardt, PhD

Ken Weingardt is a licensed psychologist in Boulder Colorado, and the Director of Training and Education for the Heroic Hearts Project. He spent nearly 20 years in the Department of Veterans Affairs, where he focused on developing and evaluating online programs for veterans and training courses for mental health providers. Ken was also a professor of Psychiatry and Behavioral Sciences at Stanford and Northwestern Medical Schools where he published extensively about how to implement innovative technologies in real-world clinical practice.

In 2020, Ken was working for a technology company in Silicon Valley developing an AI chatbot for women with Postpartum Depression. While participating in Ketamine Assisted Therapy himself, he came to the realization that he wanted to spend the third act of his career to focus on psychedelics rather than technology - on helping veterans get access to this deep transformation healing. He voted with his feet, and started working with Healing Breakthrough to help Veterans get access to MDMA through the VA.

He has since been certified by the Integrative Psychiatry Institute (IPI) as a Psychedelic Assisted Therapist, and is preparing to apply for a license as a Clinical Facilitator in Colorado. He comes to the Heroic Hearts Project with the background and experience necessary to help clinicians learn about these new ways of healing, as well as a beginner's mind and an attitude of deep gratitude and respect for all those who do this important work.

ABOUT THE AUTHOR

Meet Matt Zemon, MSc

Matt Zemon, MSc, is an educator, author, and leader in psychedelic wellness, blending academic rigor with compassionate advocacy for safer, intentional psychedelic use. He is the best-selling author of *Psychedelics for Everyone, The Beginner's Guide to Psychedelics, The Veteran's Guide to Psychedelics, and Beyond the Trip: A Journal for Psychedelic Preparation and Integration.* With a Master's degree in Psychology and Neuroscience of Mental Health from King's College London, Matt bridges ancient wisdom with modern science to help individuals navigate expansive experiences with clarity and purpose.

Beyond his writing, Matt collaborates with healthcare professionals to advance the mindful integration of psychedelics into mental health care and partners with entheogenic communities to promote risk-reduction practices and increase accessibility to these sacred tools for those seeking transformation. His work empowers veterans, spiritual seekers, and others on the path of personal growth to engage with psychedelics with care and respect.

For bulk orders, interviews, and speaking engagements, visit: www.mattzemon.com

OTHER BOOKS BY MATT ZEMON

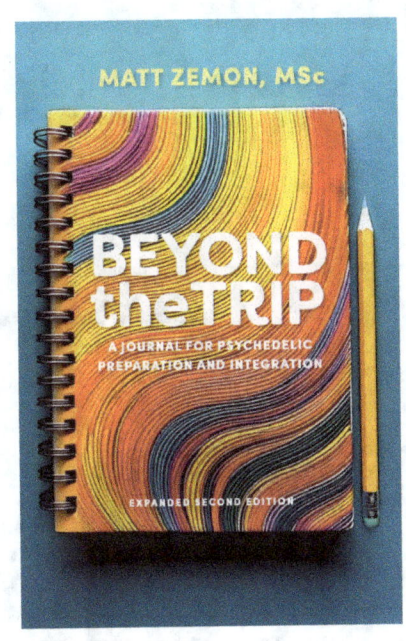

YOU ARE ENOUGH

YOU ARE WORTHY

YOU ARE LOVED

www.ingramcontent.com/pod-product-compliance
Lightning Source LLC
Chambersburg PA
CBHW071630140626
46555CB00022B/2048